DEDICATION

This book is dedicated to my loving, patient and supportive wife, Charmaine, who was born already knowing everything I strive to learn and teach. You are my inspiration and my Amazon queen. For years, I've been telling our kids to "go get your mother." Now, I get to tell others … well, sort of.

GO GET YOUR MUDA!
35 Waste-Busting Exhortations from a Professional Process Geek

Revised and expanded.

Includes thought-provoking questions and recommended next steps for each chapter.

MARK H. DAVIS

Saltcedar Publications,
Lynchburg, Virginia

Copyright © 2014 MARK H. DAVIS

All rights reserved.

No part of this book may be used or reproduced by any means, graphic, electronic, or mechanical, including photocopying, recording, taping or by any information storage retrieval system without written permission of the publisher except in the case of brief quotations embodied in critical articles and reviews.

The Author holds exclusive rights to this work.

Cover art from the iStockphoto collection on http://office.microsoft.com.

Connect with the author:
web: workflowdiagnostics.com
blog: workflowdiagnostics.wordpress.com
twitter: @workflowdx
LinkedIn: markhdavissr

ISBN: 978-0-9890491-0-8
2nd edition

Published by:
Saltcedar Publications
P.O. Box 4233
Lynchburg, VA 24502

Examples of "muda" (waste)
you will read about in this book:

- Waiting / Delays
- Unnecessary Processing
- Redundancy
- Rework
- Defects / Errors / "Fails"
- Broken Systems
- Workarounds
- Complexity
- Confusion
- Ambiguity
- Wasted Effort
- Bone-headed Ideas
- Dumb Stuff
- And others.

Look for all of these as you
make your way through.

CONTENTS

	Foreword	i
	Introduction: Where did all this waste come from?	1
1	Beware the workaround	5
2	When bad process trumps good people	9
3	Twinkle, twinkle, little On-Star, how do I get you in my car?	14
4	Tracfone: Call us for a good (long) wait time	19
5	How "smart" is your smartphone?	26
6	When "free" isn't free	29
7	20 types of medical waste (no bodily fluids involved)	32
8	At the root of it all	35
9	Everyone's favorite waste: The tax refund	37
10	School daze	39
11	Don't let Facebook get the best of you	41
12	The twisted value of the "green" bottlecap	44
13	Watery workaround: Waste-buster or waste-maker?	48
14	Systems thinking helps to sanitize the "waste"	52
15	Variety: the spice of strife	55
16	Signs of waste	58
17	One letter can be very impotant	62
18	Does this give you a warm fuzzy?	65

19	Does this give you a warm fuzzy? (Part Ooooh)	69
20	The fuel-pump sign parade	72
21	The signs of waste are everywhere	76
22	Lean times call for Lean measures	80
23	The value of change	83
24	What your process says about you	85
25	Standardize? Are you crazy?	88
26	Lather, rinse, repeat…or die	91
27	7 steps for a better burger	95
28	How to keep your S-O-P meetings from being a FLOP	99
29	(Don't) pardon the interruption	103
30	Ten Practical Tips For a Lean Workspace…or TPTFALW, for short	107
31	Let your Lean legs do the walking	113
32	How ya' doin'? How do ya' know?	120
33	Do not ask for whom the door slams…it slams for thee	123
34	Layman's definition of Lean Six Sigma	127
35	Why are we satisfied with waste?	129
	About the Author	
	Acknowledgements	

FOREWORD

I wrote this book for you.

Yes, you! The user who rolls his eyes and nibbles his sandwich while waiting for the Help Desk to live up to its name. The manager who tires of the turf wars and just wants everybody to get on the same page for once so the customer can get their order processed. The mother who wonders why it takes 90 minutes of her own time to get 5 minutes of her pediatrician's time. The consumer who knows it's not a good deal if the price of wafers is the same but the box is .3 ounces smaller. The homeowner who wants a more efficient way to rake – or blow – leaves.

I hear your cries. I feel your pain. In fact, I live it.

You call "it" something. "The bane" of your existence; "incompetence"; "just the way things are and there's nothing you can do about." Whatever. Whatever "it" is, it's not good.

I call it waste. And there *is* something we can do about it. But we never will if we don't recognize it and call it what it is.

These pages are meant to expose the waste that is around you. To spark your senses and get your blood boiling. To awaken the crusader within you that cannot rest until the world is changed. To deprive you of sleep until you are marching in the street, torch in hand, demanding an end to this madness of waste!

Are you with me?

All right! Now, go get your muda!

INTRODUCTION: WHERE DID ALL THIS WASTE COME FROM?

All of creation waits with eager longing for God to reveal His children. For creation was condemned to lose its purpose, not of its own will, but because God willed it to be so. Yet there was the hope that creation itself would one day be set free from its slavery to decay and would share the glorious freedom of the children of God. ~The Apostle Paul in his letter to the church at Rome (Romans 8:19-21)

Waste is everywhere.

Don't think so? Ask yourself these questions:

- The last time you shaved (your face or your legs, or both I guess), how easy was it to get all of the shaving cream off of your hands and onto your skin? How efficient was the transfer of the cream? How much did you wash down the drain when it became obvious any more effort would be futile? And when you shaved, how many overlapping strokes were required? Did you shave the same spot once, twice or three times for good measure?

- Like yogurt? Wish you had a better tool than a spoon with which to scrape it all up? Find yourself scraping, and scraping, and scraping to get every last drop of your favorite flavor out of the cup? Or are you like my 7-year-old daughter, who discards the spoon in favor of her tongue, and transfers much of the remainder to her face?
- Did you rake leaves last fall? Whether you used a leaf blower or a rake, did you feel like you were moving the same leaves again and again, sometimes back and forth over the same spot, struggling with repeated jabs or strokes as your shoulders, arms and back burned with pain? Did you swear off the job and hire a yard man (read: "neighborhood teen-ager")?
- Do you ever drive anywhere? Encounter any stop lights? Ever stare incredulously at a red light and wonder why you aren't moving since no one else is, either?
- Have you ever gone to the doctor or the ER? Did you walk right in, see the doctor, get your diagnosis and treatment and flow right through? Or, like every other creature on the planet, did you wait repeatedly and give the same information to several different people, and then go to a specialist, therapist or pharmacy and repeat the same information and experience?

Okay, I think I caught you nodding (in agreement, not in slumber). You recognized yourself somewhere, perhaps everywhere, in these examples. Which means you encountered or endured waste. You may have even caused it.

So where does all this waste come from? Why does it happen? Why is it omnipresent?

The Bible tells us that man fell into corruption when he disobeyed God. But he alone does not bear the consequences of this sin. Creation itself – every living thing, every natural system, the very conditions that define our existence – is now also marred by decay and imperfection. In fact, the Apostle Paul tells us that creation groans for release from its prison of futility and to be restored to its perfect, harmonious, purposeful state with the return of Jesus Christ No more tears. No more pain. No more death.

No more waste.

Until then, we are stuck with it.

But that doesn't mean we can't fight it. God gave us minds that can analyze, innovate and confront the challenges of waste. He gave us insights into orderly systems design and conservation, the underpinnings of Lean; He blessed us with discoveries in mathematics and logic that form the foundation of Six Sigma. With these and other powerful methods, we can continually shave the waste that accumulates in our lives. All it takes is a decision to do so.

We may be destined for failure if perfection is our goal, but we are doomed to mediocrity if we fail to pursue it. The sight of the peak is what beckons and inspires us, leading us to heights we would never have achieved had we never made the summit our target.

This book is all about that climb toward the summit, a relentless and intentional journey that is fueled not by a whimsical dream of operational utopia, but by the unfolding revelation that progress is not only possible, but mandatory. We must demand it of ourselves; we must model it for others; and we must require it in every professional engagement. We must reach for the sky.

So fight waste, we must – knowing that if we don't, we have not only lost time, money and resources, but opportunity, purpose and hope.

Adam and Eve plunged us headlong into this mess. But

God has given us ways to dig out. He has ordained us to be waste-busters. So let's get started.

-1-
BEWARE THE WORKAROUND

I hate to admit it, but my plumbing is starting to fail.

No, not my personal plumbing – that would be another issue entirely, and one I'd be more likely to share with my physician than with an international audience.

The topic here is the plumbing in my house, which is nearing 40 years old. Nearly every faucet drips no matter how tightly you cinch down the knobs. I'm sure I've seen a handy gasket kit that would fix this, but, you know that would mean I'd have to go all the way to the hardware store, find the right item, pay for it, bring it home, read the instructions, install several sets of these, realize to my horror that I've forgotten to shut off the water supply, frantically clean up the mess I've caused, say some things I shouldn't and pretty much ruin a Saturday afternoon.

As former President Bush (the elder) would say, "Not gonna do it; not gonna do it."

What I am willing to do, though, is find a workaround. And this I've done for our peskiest faucet, the one in our master bath shower.

Tired of hearing the constant drip, I placed a plastic mop

pail in the floor of the shower. This doesn't stop the drip, but it does cure the intense frustration I've had that with every drop, money and a precious resource are going down the drain.

The pail is just the perfect size, too; over a day's time, it fills to about halfway, at which point we're ready to use the shower again. But what should we do with the water we've "saved?"

I put my mind to work on this problem. Hmmm ... I know, we could water the plants on the back porch. No, the coming winter will put a damper on that idea (so to speak). How about washing the dishes? Oooh, okay, bad idea. Certainly there's a use for this perfectly good water. We certainly don't want to waste it, do we?

Being a "process" guy, I came up with the master plan – whenever we flush the toilet, we'll lift the tank cover and pour the "saved" water into the tank as it refills, replace the pail and repeat again later ... and pat ourselves on the back for being such wise stewards of money and resources.

Whew. Problem solved.

Really?

OK, not really. To solve one problem, I've really created another – a whole new process designed to catch the waste and defects from the first one. What about all the time and effort I'm wasting with this workaround process? Sure, I feel good about myself, but wouldn't it be easier to just fix the real problem? After all, as they say, "quality matters" ... even at home.

I know one thing, I am getting a little tired of moving all the nice trinkets off the toilet cover just to transfer the water from the pail to the tank. Maybe I should just relocate the candles, decorative soaps, magazines and other articles to another area so we can keep our workaround going.

No way my wife is going to go for that. Is there a plumber in the house?

_____QUESTIONS TO CONSIDER_____

- Can you relate with this story?
- Do you build "workarounds" like these?
- What are some examples?
- What types of waste do workarounds create?

NEXT STEPS

- Identify at least one workaround at home or work.
- Determine and fix the true source of the problem.
- Eliminate the workaround process.
- Notify others.
- Clarify that workarounds are not acceptable replacements for properly running systems and real fixes.
- The next time you are tempted to implement a workaround, stop yourself. Apply a temporary fix if you must, and assign a deadline for the true fix.

-2-
WHEN BAD PROCESS TRUMPS GOOD PEOPLE

What do people tend to say when they have a bad experience?

"Those people are incompetent!"

"Nobody in there knows what they're doing."

"It's so hard to get good help these days…"

Admit it, you've probably said all of the above at some point. OK, I'm guilty, too.

Our tendency is to blame people for a bad service experience, when oftentimes, the process is the real problem. They're just trapped in it. Well-intentioned and highly trained souls can appear to be circus monkeys when a bad process takes over.

I had just such an experience recently, involving one bad process spread across multiple silos and shared by several friendly, eager-to-help individuals. A regular barrel of monkeys.

It all started on February 19, when I sold an old van for cash. First thing I did was log on to the Department of Motor Vehicles (DMV) web site for my state and report the vehicle as being sold. That was actually pretty easy. Great process.

Imagine my surprise when, a month later, I received a registration renewal notice in the mail for that same vehicle. I called the DMV to clear up any confusion.

"Sir, we do show that vehicle as sold."

"OK, so why am I receiving a renewal notice?"

"Your old plates are still active."

"I'm not using those anymore."

"Then you need to de-activate them. I can do that for you now."

Thank goodness.

"You have 9 months to re-activate them if you wish. Is there anything else I can help you with?"

"No, that's it today. Thanks."

"OK. Now, you'll also want to let your locality know that you sold this vehicle. Otherwise, they will send you a personal property tax bill again this year."

"Hey, thanks for that reminder. I'll let them know. Whom do I call for that?"

"You'll need to call the city Treasurer's office. They'll take care of it for you."

"Thanks. I'll call them now."

So I did. Then the real fun started.

"You've reached the Treasurer's office. Our office hours are 8:30 a.m. to 4:30 p.m. weekdays, except legal holidays. If you'd like to leave a message for (Ralph), press 1; if you'd like to leave a message for (Shirley), press 2. Thanks, and have a great day."

Hmmm. Our Treasurer's office consists of an automated phone screener and two individuals. I flipped a mental coin and pressed 1.

"You've reached Ralph. I can't take your call, but please

leave a message and I'll call you right back. If you need immediate help, please call our main number."

That made a whole bunch of sense. Call the main number and get right back where I started? Avoiding that vicious cycle, I left (Ralph) a message. Thirty minutes later, (Shirley) called me back.

"I'm covering (Ralph's) voice mails today. Can I help you?"

"Yes. Thanks for calling back. I need to report the sale of a vehicle. Can you help me with that?"

"No, we don't handle that here in this office."

"Oh, OK. So, who does?"

"That's the Billing and Collections office. I believe they would be the ones for that. They send out the bills. I'll transfer you over to them, if you like."

"OK ... thanks."

Still with me? Good. Try to keep up. It just gets better.

"Billing and Collections. How can I help you?"

"I need to report the sale of a vehicle. Can you help me with that?"

"Uhhh, no, we don't do that here, sir. You need to discuss that with the Commissioner's Office. They issue the tax bills. If you can hang on, I'll try to transfer you. If we get cut off, here's the number ..."

"OK ... thanks."

At this point, I was actually thinking I should have just kept the thing.

"Commissioner's Office. How can I help you?"

"I need to report the sale of a vehicle. Can you help me with that?"

"Yes, we can do that." (Yes!) "What was the make and model of the vehicle?"

"It was a 1997 Chevy Express Van."

"Hold on a minute; let me check... Would that have been the 1997 Chevrolet Truck G30 Van?"

"Yes, that's the one."

"OK. Well, we actually show that it's been sold already, on February 19 of this year."

"Why, yes it has. How did you know?"

Kicker:

"The DMV told us."

"You mean ... but they were the ones ... why didn't they ... Never mind." SMH.

"Is there anything else I can help you with today, sir?"

"No thanks. I've had enough help for one day."

Simple communication. Sometimes, that's all we need. It can turn a ridiculous, redundant process into a finely oiled machine. Left hand? Let me introduce you to the right hand. You guys need to move in together. You already share a shirt and a steering wheel. You peel bananas together. How about talking more often? (sign language, of course)

In this case, the left hand (DMV) didn't even know what the left hand had done. Took the right hand to tell me that. Now that's a new one. Right hand, please tell the left hand what the left hand has been doing. Left hand, please pay attention so that next time you'll know what you've done.

What's that? Now that's just rude. I may not know sign language, but I know it takes more than 1 finger...

Time to wrap up. This is getting out of hand, so to speak. Like I said, it's so hard to get good help nowadays...

_____QUESTIONS TO CONSIDER_____

- Have you had similar experiences?
- What made you the angriest: Time wasted? ... Bad instructions? ... Unclear process? ... Discourteous reps? ... Lack of communication? ... All of the above?
- Did you express your frustration to the organization, or to other acquaintances?
- Why do such breakdowns exist?
- Can they be prevented? What can we do about them?

_____NEXT STEPS_____

- Identify gaps in communication between different groups, functions or departments at work.
- Assemble a cross-functional team and review the current process (list or map out the steps).
- Collectively, design a new process that ensures communication and role clarity.
- Re-evaluate after a short time.

-3-
TWINKLE, TWINKLE, LITTLE ON-STAR, HOW DO I GET YOU IN MY CAR?

The commercials are compelling.

"Hello. This is On-Star. How can I help you?" they begin.

"I'm caught in the jaws of a shark and I'm all out of mace. Can you help me?" the suffering subscriber pleads.

"Just relax, sir," the advisor says calmly. "I'll send a remote zap to the shark's nervous system, thus rendering it unconscious so you can escape. Do you also need us to beam down a life preserver and first-aid kit?"

"Yes, that would be great. Thanks so much, On-Star. You truly are a life-saver…"

OK, so this is a little exaggerated, but you get the point. If you have On-Star, you undoubtedly have a sense of security that others do not have – an eye in the sky, a benevolent big brother, a guardian angel. But for others, like me, who are trying to get it, the On-Star experience can be quite painful.

Let me explain.

I recently purchased a 2004 Yukon with an On-Star system … that needs to be activated. I've been itching to get that thing turned on. I imagine my wife driving our kids around with a shield of protection around her, an impenetrable force field fending off all evil. I envision myself using the navigation system so I'll never get lost again (right) ... the hands-free phone service so I can play Captain Kirk on the bridge of the Enterprise. I ache for the ability to unlock the doors when we (I) inevitably lock our keys inside. I dream...

So far, my dream has been a nightmare. It's been one roadblock after another as I've spun my wheels trying to crank that baby up (all puns intended). All of its reassuring potential lies just out of my reach, the pleasant icons that adorn my rear-view mirror taunting me with every glance.

Here's a blow-by-blow account of my unsuccessful attempts to tap into the power of On-Star:

First, I consulted the On-Star web site, where there was a promotion for three months of free service upon reactivation. That sounded great, so ...

I tried to "pre-register" by entering the vehicle VIN, but the drop-down form only listed vehicles back to 2006. "For older vehicles, click here," it said. So, I did...

As soon as I released the mouse, I know I heard somebody, somewhere, say, "Sucker!" When you "click here," you go back to the original promotion page and it's unclear what to do next. It's a vicious cycle, probably meant to discourage owners of older vehicles. I, however, pressed on ...

And pressed the numbers on my cell phone. I called the On-Star number shown on the web site – 1-888-ONSTAR1. A nice lady (recorded) told me the number was for dealerships only and that I should call a different number – 1-888-4ONSTAR – if I was a consumer. I pressed on again...

I called 1-888-4ONSTAR and talked to a customer service agent. She advised that the only way to know if the system could be activated was to contact On-Star from the vehicle. The only way to determine if the system could be activated was to call an advisor from the system itself. The issue was whether the system was analog or digital. Basically, if analog – it's junk; if digital – there's hope. To check the system, I should press the blue button twice to connect to an advisor, or press the red emergency button and ask for an advisor for re-activation. With strident steps, out to the vehicle I went...

I pressed the blue button. A sales pitch ensued. "Beth Williams," a pleasant-sounding On-Star advisor, talked about all the nice features of On-Star (nothing about sharks, though). During the sales pitch, she said to press the blue button again to contact an advisor to activate the system. This agreed with the agent's instructions, so...

I pressed the blue button again. "Contacting On-Star," I was told. Then, I waited. And waited. And waited. Every 5 seconds or so, I'd get a beep that would keep me waiting hopefully for an advisor. No dice. After about 30 seconds of beeps, the system declared, "Unable to contact On-Star agent," then it cut off. No problem. I went to Plan B...

The red emergency button! This would certainly get me somewhere, I thought. After all, this was becoming a true service emergency. I pressed the red button without a shade of guilt and immediately heard, "On-Star system not activated," followed by this stunning instruction: "Please press the blue On-Star button to speak with an advisor about activation." Arrrggghhh!

Like a desperate dummy, I pressed the blue button again. Maybe it was just a glitch the first time. Maybe I just held my mouth wrong. Maybe ... not. Same result. "Beth Williams," beeps, failure, disconnect. Frustration...

Out of options, I called On-Star again. I explained my

situation, again. I described what I'd done that didn't work. I begged for help. (Wasn't this the system that could send an ambulance to an unconscious driver just by telepathy or vibes or something?) I was put on hold so I could be transferred to "that department." Grrr...

A short time later, the agent returned. "Still there?" Yes ... barely. We reviewed the facts again. She thanked me for holding, then transferred me (for real this time) to a technical service agent. Hope breathed...

I took a deep breath and reviewed the facts, one more time (I was getting pretty good at it by then). She asked if my system was analog or digital. I said that's what we were trying to determine in the first place. She said it was likely analog, since it wouldn't connect to On-Star when the blue button was pressed. But, it could also be due to their own system upgrades, which were creating "higher than normal call volumes" for the On-Star advisors. That's reassuring, I thought – is this the system I'm supposed to count on if my Yukon's teetering on the side of a cliff? I was left with three options: 1) Consult the owner's manual. It might know if the system is analog or digital; 2) Call the dealership. They'll know if the system is analog or digital. 3) Keep trying and hope that the "higher than normal call volumes" are the culprit. An orderly numbers guy, I chose option 1...

The owner's manual knew everything about my system ... except whether it was digital or analog. Hello, option 2...

I called the dealership and tried to sound cheery. I managed to maintain that disposition when they told me they weren't sure which system I had (analog or digital), but the service department said some 2004's were upgradeable ... at a friendly cost of $214. After telling them I'd have to think about it, I prayed for option 3 to work...

Predictably, it didn't, or at least it hasn't yet. It's still the blue button of disappointment. I'll be pressing that blue button periodically for the next few days, though. On second thought — if you are related to an On-Star advisor, married to one, have one in your Sunday School class, or just happen to meet one in the store ("Beth Williams" maybe), can you have them call me, instead? Maybe they can help me unlock my car. In the midst of the ordeal, I locked my keys in there.

_____QUESTIONS TO CONSIDER_____

- Have you had similar experiences?
- What types of "muda" were present?
- How did you feel? Did you tell anyone?

_____NEXT STEPS_____

- Review your customer enrollment or application process.
- Follow the flow. Include advertisements, phone greetings, billboards – anything you use to reach out, any entry point.
- Is the flow smooth and simple? Consistent? Customer-friendly? Void of unnecessary hand-offs, gaps and "dropped balls?" Or does it run people around in circles?
- If necessary, take steps to improve this important workflow for your customers. They're talking about you.

-4-
TRACFONE: CALL US FOR A GOOD (LONG) WAIT TIME

I'm aggravated if I have an experience with a company that does not match the marketing. Aren't you? It's like a company has broken a promise, fooled us and then laughed as they took our money. That's why I choose to blog about such experiences – because quality matters, and companies need to know that.

This rant is about Tracfone. (I feel the earth tilting as millions of readers nod in agreement.) Tracfone is marketed as a reliable, affordable, no-frills option to costly and complicated contracts. "The phone that puts you in control."

Unless you want to reactivate.

Overall, I have to say that my past experience with Tracfone was positive. I still recommend their pay-as-you-go cellular service for those who are budget-minded or want a cell phone "just in case." It's a great choice for these customers.

That's where my praise ends. It comes to a screeching, terrifying halt if and when you have to get on the phone with them. I've always thought it was ironic that many telecommunications giants – Verizon, Comcast and others – have absolutely deplorable call centers, where you're blessed if you don't have to wait forever and you're actually able to communicate with the off-shore agent (not an ethnic bias here, just an acknowledgement that good communication is essential to good service). In many of my Tracfone experiences, they have failed both tests.

Like today. All I wanted to do was reactivate a Tracfone I've had for about 2 years. (I deactivated it last year when the kids kept wasting all the minutes browsing and texting.) I need something I can give my kids when they go to ball practice, dance rehearsal, youth groups and other activities and just need to call for a ride. I just need enough minutes for the kids to say, "I'm ready," a dozen times a month.

I need a Tracfone.

So off to the web site I go. There's actually a tab to activate a phone, so I start there. It shows all the phones I've had with them, lets me choose one, asks for the SIM number and then ... tells me there is a problem and I need to call the customer service line for help.

I should have known better. I've had other experiences with that process, and they were never pretty. Shaky system, noisy background, lots of hold time, propensity to fail. Here we go again, and again, and again...

At first, everything appeared to be going smoothly. The automated attendant led me right to a reactivation selection, where another upbeat (automated) agent proceeded to help me reactivate my phone (so I thought). Five minutes into the call, however, he (it) asked if I had purchased an airtime card. (Why would I have? My phone wasn't even active.) "No," I replied. He politely told me to call back when I had, and hung up. That was it. No apologies, no see-you-laters. I love it when machines are nice and rude all at the same time.

Too far into this to give up, I determined to buy an airtime card, even though my phone still shows 189 unused minutes from before. I found a great deal at walmart.com (beat the Tracfone price by 11 cents, I think). With the PIN for 60 minutes of Tracfone airtime in hand, I called my nice friends at Tracfone back. I got to the same question about the airtime card and … this time, the auto attendant handed me off to a real-live person. Uh-oh…

"Thank you for calling Tracfone. This is (Betty). How can I help you today?"

"I need to reactivate my Tracfone and I've bought an airtime card. Can you help me do that?"

Nothing.

"Thank you for calling Tracfone. This is (Betty). How can I help you today?"

"I need to reactivate my Tracfone and I've bought an airtime card. Can you help me do that."

Nothing.

"Hello? … "Hello?" … "Hello?"

Nothing. Then I heard hold music for about 30 seconds. (Betty) came back.

"Thank you for calling Tracfone. This is (Betty). How can I help you today?"

"I need to reactivate my Tracfone and I've bought an airtime card. Can you help me do that?"

Finally, "Yes, I can help you do that."

Whew.

First, she asked for the phone number of the cell.

"I'm sorry, sir. That number is invalid."

"That's the number it tells me it is. Are you sure?"

"That's what my system says, sir."

"OK, what else can I tell you?"

"Please give me the serial number and I'll check that."

I gave her the number. She asked me to repeat it, slowly. Then, she asked me to wait as she entered it into her system. What? She wasn't typing it as I read it? She was writing it down and then typing it in. Wow. Thankfully, it checked out.

"Now can you please tell me the SIM number of the phone? And please read it slowly for me."

It took 60 seconds to read the 16-digit number.

"Please allow me a few moments to enter it into my system."

Wow again.

"I'm sorry sir, my system is saying that number is invalid. Can you read it to me again? And please read it slowly."

Deep, cleansing breath.

"Sure. The number on the phone screen is …"

"Thank you, sir. Please allow me a few moments to enter it into my system again."

Pregnant pause. I'm wondering what else I could/should be doing. Does the car need washing and waxing today?

"I'm sorry sir, my system is still saying that number is invalid. Please may I put you on hold while I communicate with my supervisor?"

Oh no, the dreaded "supervisor!" I had no choice. Into "supervisor" purgatory I went … and there I stayed for the next 35 minutes. Every two minutes (Betty) would come back on and say,

"Thank you for holding, sir, but I'm still trying to communicate with my supervisor about this problem. Can I place you on hold for another two minutes?"

I don't know why, but 10 times in a row I said "yes." I

guess I had too much time invested to get nothing out of it. Then, disaster struck.

"Sir, our system has gone down and we are bringing it back up. This may take a few minutes. May I place you on hold for another two minutes?"

"OK."

I think I was drooling, my mouth hung open in amazement for so long.

"Thank you, sir."

If the "supervisor" was purgatory and the "system down" was a disaster, the next event was an exponential Titanic.

"Sir, I've been told for you to call us back in one hour's time. Thank you."

"I'm sorry? What would you like for me to do?"

Nothing. No sound. No static. Just an eerie stillness. Then …

"If you'd like to make a call, please hang up and dial the number again…"

Static. Fuzz. Shock.

"If you'd like to make a call, please hang up and dial the number again…"

Iceberg city. They had cut me off. And now, a different machine was giving me more politely rude instructions.

Thankfully, other tasks pulled me away. Like waxing my legs. Chewing on aluminum foil. Sticking needles into my eyes. You know, pleasant things. But, I did manage to call Tracfone back a few hours later. This time, I got to speak with "Talia."

"I'm sorry sir, my system is saying that SIM number is invalid. Please may I put you on hold while I communicate with my supervisor?"

"Sure. Why not?"

"Thank you, sir."

Ten minutes passed. I reluctantly gave permission to be on hold several times. Then the ordeal ended not with a gunshot, but with a small fiber optic cable piercing my eyeball.

"Thank you for holding, sir. I've been told that we need to send you another SIM card for your phone. This should take three to five days. Can I have your mailing address, please?"

I didn't know whether to laugh or cry. I was actually relieved that my lengthy quest was ending. With a mixture of shock and awe, I mumbled my address and the call ended mercifully.

We have amazing technology. We have smartphones that can essentially drive our cars, cook our food and wash our clothes. We have immediate access to everything from local restaurant menus to satellite images of Hong Kong , but I have to wait three to five days to get a new SIM card so my kids can call me when practice is over. So, what about tomorrow's practice? Maybe I'll call them back and ask for overnight shipping.

Naaahhh. I can wait. And that's not something you hear me say very often.

_____QUESTIONS TO CONSIDER_____

- Have you had similar customer service experiences? What was your reaction? Did you complain?
- What types of "muda" are created by these experiences? Does one of them include cancellation of service – essentially rendering the entire episode wasteful?
- Do you tend to avoid companies that waste your time?
- What are some ways to improve these experiences?

NEXT STEPS

- Review your company or department customer service processes. How much time and effort does it take to fulfill customer requests?
- Identify areas of workarounds, complexity, frequent failures or downtime. Strive for simplicity and first-time success.
- Eliminate redundancies and unnecessary steps that your customer would not find valuable.
- Define the "dream state" for your customers and take steps to build it.

-5-
HOW "SMART" IS YOUR SMARTPHONE

A few years ago, I made an investment in my business productivity: I bought a smartphone.

What a revolution in productivity this was supposed to be. I could surf the web, manage my calendar, keep up with contacts – and make phone calls, of course – right from the palm of my hand.

But the real beauty of it all, to me at least, was that I could read my e-mails without being at my desk. I'd never miss an important response, a meeting request or an anniversary reminder. That gave me the chills. I had always (secretly) envied colleagues whose Blackberries buzzed across the conference room table every time they received a message. How busy and important they sounded! Now, it was my turn to join the club of the productive elite.

Recently, however, I've started to question the wisdom of my smartphone purchase, at least when it comes to reading those sacred e-mails. I seem to spend most of my time discovering new things my supposed "smart" phone can't do ... like open various attachments, follow certain links, access different discussion boards, utilize a business logo in my signature, file e-mails in categorized folders or give me a fast way to type out a response without embarrassing spelling or spacing issues. Now, instead of opening an e-mail once, then either responding, filing or deleting the message, I open it multiple times – once on my phone and then at least once again on my computer – which means I read it multiple times, just to make sure I didn't miss anything. On top of all this, I've started to notice that I rarely get e-mails from real people. I mostly get subscriptions, reminders, announcements, etc. – nothing that can't wait. Yet, I let them interrupt whatever I'm doing at the moment they arrive. There's that buzz – I can't ignore it – it might be something important!

I shudder to admit it, but I now believe that my smartphone has actually hurt my productivity and made me a less efficient, more redundant worker. Given all of these shortcomings, the "smartest" way to manage my e-mails is – you guessed it – from my computer.

If it wasn't for the hint of euphoria I experience every time that buzzer goes off on my hip… I'd turn the thing off. This may be one redundancy I'll have to live with for awhile.

_____QUESTIONS TO CONSIDER_____

- What has your "smartphone" experience been like? Has it improved your productivity or generated new "muda?"
- Is new technology always more efficient? Or, does it sometimes create waste of its own?
- Are you cognizant of this new waste, or too infatuated with the new gadget to notice?

NEXT STEPS

- Adjust your smartphone settings to minimize unnecessary notifications.
- Strive for handling e-mails one time (only). Avoid opening and reopening.
- For accuracy and clarity, compose important e-mails and replies at the computer.
- Avoid downloading and storing the same files on your phone AND your computer.

-6-
WHEN "FREE" ISN'T FREE

I was in a pediatrics office recently when I noticed an interesting sign: "Free Wi-Fi."

Initially I thought, "Wow! What a cool service! Bring your laptop and surf away while you wait for the doctor to call your child back."

Neat!

I looked around the waiting room to see if any patrons were taking advantage of this "free" service. While I didn't notice any, I did notice several taking advantage of other novelties. One young lady stared with wonder into a giant aquarium; a young lad with a runny nose played with an old-fashioned car garage at the toy depot; still another flipped through the pages of a youth-oriented magazine in the reading center. Parents fiddled with their respective electronic gadgets (phones mostly, no laptops), occasionally glancing in their children's directions, assured that they were safely occupied by their curiosities.

What a nice place to come and play! And you can even web-surf, too! What more could you want?

How about a little time with the doctor, and soon?

While offering wi-fi to patients is certainly cutting-edge, modern and differentiating (for the moment, at least), it is definitely not "free" – for anyone, really. First of all, for a patient to have time to surf the office's internet, they'll have to be WAITING. Isn't the patient's time (and their parents' time, in this case) worth anything anymore? In healthcare, we've reached a dangerous point where we only think the doctor's time is valuable. Don't get me wrong – it definitely is – but this doesn't mean the patients' time is "free."

Nor is the wi-fi service "free" to the clinic. Think about it. If patients are waiting, they're not getting examined. If they're not getting examined, there's nothing to charge for. The process is backlogged, and so is the clinic's capacity, productivity and profitability. Isn't the whole point to provide a valuable service (healthcare) to as many people as we can, and get paid for it so we can provide it to others? (Maybe this is why so many offices have gone to collecting co-pays up front. Just sayin'.)

Some time ago, a dental practice in our area built a new, state-of-the-art office with all the modern conveniences you could imagine. Here's a description taken directly from their promotional flier (note the first feature listed): "spacious waiting areas, quiet reading nooks, wireless internet access, ample parking, movies throughout the office, Playstation Game Console at every treatment chair and even a private game room!" All I can think is, "How long do they plan for people to be at this office, anyway? And whose money did they use to construct this dental Disneyland?" Now I know why my dental premiums are so high.

This waiting is killing us, and it's costing us more and more money every day. I've even been in offices that not only have one waiting room, but two! And the magazine selection and big screen TV's were even more plentiful in the second than in the first. Now, I know what everyone is thinking. "As long as they're waiting, we might as well give them something to do." How about eliminating the wait instead? There are ways to do that. And I'm sure the patients won't mind.

I believe we need a major paradigm shift in healthcare. I'm not talking about legislative reform; as I've written before, I don't believe that is the complete answer for our woes. We, of all professionals, should be able to put our customers first, value their time at least as highly as our own, and design work processes that run efficiently without sacrificing quality. This is infinitely more valuable than any "freebies" we could ever offer.

_____QUESTIONS TO CONSIDER_____

- Do you normally have to wait at your doctor's office?
- How long?
- How does this make you feel?
- Would you rather see the doctor or enjoy more "freebies?"
- Do your customers wait?
- Do you take steps to make their wait more bearable, or try to reduce the wait?

_____NEXT STEPS_____

- Tell your doctor that punctuality is a 2-way street.
- Identify all the times your customers have to wait.
- Ask "why" continually. Attack the reasons one by one.

-7-
20 TYPES OF MEDICAL WASTE (NO BODILY FLUIDS INVOLVED)

When people hear the term "medical waste," they probably think of bloody bandages, soiled linens or used syringes. But there are other forms of waste that are more pre-dominant in the medical office that have nothing to do with the physical by-products of procedures, tests or treatment.

The most prevalent form of medical waste is actually process waste – inefficiency, redundancy, rework, unnecessary work and other forms of "waste" that steal time, money and resources out from under our noses. One study even estimates that half of every dollar spent in healthcare is actually wasted (PricewaterhouseCoopers, *The Price of Excess*, April 2008). That translates to more than a trillion dollars!

Tragically, we've learned to live with much of this waste, though we complain about it constantly. We even design our facilities to accommodate it. Ever hear of a waiting room?

Lean divides waste into 7 basic categories: waiting, defects, overprocessing / redundancy, unnecessary transport, unnecessary motion, overutilization / underutilization and excessive inventory. Once you learn how to "see" waste in a healthcare setting, you start to see it everywhere.

Following is a list of 20 examples of waste from the typical medical office. See if any of these are familiar:

1. Waiting anywhere ... the front window, waiting room, exam room, lab, scheduler, etc.
2. Patients on hold
3. Bringing in more patients than can be seen at one time (creates wait)
4. Multiple waiting rooms (more space for more people to wait)
5. Batching claims, dictation, etc. (creates waiting until they all are done)
6. Illegible Rx or notes
7. Rejected claims (errors / missing info)
8. Waiting for outside documentation
9. Late arrivals (patient or staff)
10. Cancellations / reschedules (various reasons)
11. Redundant forms / questions
12. Redundant entries of same information in multiple places (e.g. form & EMR)
13. Unnecessary tests, appointments, labs or Rx
14. Results not communicated to the patient.
15. Walking back & forth from window file / supply cabinet for each patient
16. Calling patient back, then sending back out
17. Walking from patient room to office or supply room for every patient (excessive movement)
18. "Busy-ness" (underutilization)
19. No lunch or potty break (overutilization)
20. Storing forms or supplies you never use

This is just a sample of what's out there. Obviously, the opportunities for improvement in healthcare are substantial.

This is why I believe the first step in healthcare reform should be a re-engineering of the workflows from the ground up – starting with the general practitioners and branching out to every variety and specialty of medical care we have. The benefits would be enormous – to the health of our nation and the health of our citizens.

QUESTIONS TO CONSIDER

- What other types of waste do you notice at your doctor's office? Have you learned to just accept this as normal?
- Does everyone seem to be working as hard as they can? Why does the process take so long?
- Do you ever complain about waiting (or other types of waste)? What is the typical response?
- Do you notice waste at other types of businesses? How about at your own?

NEXT STEPS

- At your next visit, tell your doctor how long you are willing to wait. Ask if no waiting is an option.
- Ask your doctor to keep his/her time commitments.
- Encourage your doctor to involve his staff in a review of office procedures. Share your experience or observations.
- Walk around and observe the work at your own place of business. Note the types of waste you see. Ask why they are occurring. Identify at least one example that can be eliminated with minimal effort or approvals.

-8-
AT THE ROOT OF IT ALL

Waste is kind of like a cancer – left unchecked it likes to spread out until it takes over the body.

I'm working with a doctor's office right now where some of the physicians don't like to complete their visit notes until days or even weeks later.

Just this simple act of waiting – a key type of waste – creates a lot of disturbances in other parts of the business.

- First, the office can't bill for the visit until the note is done, so it holds up the revenue stream.
- Second, other diagnostic tests cannot be performed until the note is done, so it holds up patient care.
- Third, the doctor may not remember the visit clearly or completely when he finally does his note. There's the potential for errors.
- Finally, someone in the office has to constantly remind the doctors to complete their charts. There's rework and wasted time.

This is a great example of how waste can impact a business. And where did it all start? With one decision to not finish the work until later.

Why was that decision made? Other patients were waiting in the exam rooms. They had been pushed downstream for the doctor to process as quickly as he could. Inventory (patients) had been allowed to build up. And more were being assembled (for lack of better word) out in the waiting room. Truncating the work was the noble thing to do. But in a way, it was also self-defeating. Doctors complained of losing their evenings and weekends to charting. Relationships at home were suffering.

What a waste.

Overproduction, "push" processing – those simple acts of "waste" were what led to all the other impacts. Waste had grown all over the place, like a sprawling patch of weeds.

Waste proliferates.

If you don't address it, it will consume you like kudzu.

_____QUESTIONS TO CONSIDER_____

- Look at the work that you do. Do you leave "loose ends" undone until later?
- What is the impact of this delay? On you? On others? On your business or group?

_____NEXT STEPS_____

- Identify opportunities to get entire projects/tasks done before starting the next (a key Lean principle known as "one-piece flow.")
- Measure the impact on your personal productivity, accuracy and timeliness. Did they improve, or suffer?

-9-
EVERYONE'S FAVORITE WASTE: THE TAX REFUND

I heard a shocking statement during a commercial for one of the leading tax filing services recently.

"Your tax refund is probably the largest single check you'll receive this year. Don't trust some no-name, over-the-counter software to create an accurate tax return for you. Rely on our trusted application to get you the biggest refund!"

First of all, if your tax refund is your biggest payout this year, you need to change careers.

And then you need to make some major adjustments to your withholdings.

Many of us are excited by the prospect of the tax return. It's free money, we think. An extra bonus we didn't work for. Pennies from heaven (figuratively, hopefully). A small ship that comes in every year at this time.

Wrong.

It's actually the opposite of all those things. We did work for it – that's why we're getting it back, after all – but we decided to lend it to the government, interest-free, out of the goodness of our hearts, and then we break our own necks to get it back, under the threat of unintended errors and dreaded audits. Furthermore, those of us with complicated returns probably pay for the "premium" software or hire a CPA to handle the filing process. So this is definitely not free money coming our way. It's really just lazy management of money we should have had in the first place, but chose to receive later so we could have a hollow celebration and make a down payment on a new car or bedroom suite ... thus compounding the problem.

So, while I'm always reluctant to add to the types of waste categorized within Lean, I must expand the list by at least this one category: unnecessary, interest-free loans to the IRS.

Tax refunds, for short.

Then again, I guess we have to have something to make the tax-filing process bearable.

Avoidance of fines and imprisonment just doesn't have the same appeal.

QUESTIONS TO CONSIDER

- Do you strive for and anticipate a big refund each year?
- Do you see this as prudent or wasteful?
- Do you consider the waiting, lost interest and intricate steps taken to optimize the refund to be "muda?"

NEXT STEPS

- Consider adjusting your wage withholdings to pay only as much tax as you owe – and receive more in your paycheck now.

-10-
SCHOOL DAZE

August 27, 2012

Well, it's that time of year again, and the kids are finally back at school. (woo-hoo!)

For us, that means 6 kids going to 4 different schools (if you include my youngest daughter's pre-school).

It didn't take long for waste to show up in the school system's process. (Of course I'm going to notice that.)

First of all, the buses were supposed to come 10 minutes EARLIER than last year, but they actually have been coming 10 minutes LATER. Do you know how much wasted time that means for our family? (How about 100 minutes per day!)

We're not sure if they're just running late, or if the schedule was wrong. So we're still getting up early just in case.

On the first day of class, my kids brought home duplicates of the same forms that we completed at registration ... for each class! They all want the same information about us – name, address, e-mail, phone number, etc. It's obvious that the departments don't talk to each other.

Sadly, my 6th-grader summed it all up when he said, "Middle school is boring."

That sounds like the biggest waste of all – my 11-year-old isn't being challenged in his new grade.

I share all this to encourage you to look for waste in your businesses – wasted time, redundancy, or even wasted days.

If you have trouble finding it, just ask your customers. They'll tell you.

And if you need help getting rid of it, just contact me. I'll probably be on the phone with the school system, but you can leave me a message and I'll call you back.

QUESTIONS TO CONSIDER

- What types of waste were discussed?
- What types of frustrations do you have with your kids' school system?
- How much of your frustration is due to waste that seems inane, persistent and simple to solve?
- Do you ever express frustration? What is the response?
- Why does this waste exist and perpetuate?

NEXT STEPS

- In the space below (or elsewhere), list a few suggestions you'd like to share with your school system:

_____

_____

- Donate a copy of this book to your local school principal or superintendent.

-11-
DON'T LET FACEBOOK GET THE BEST OF YOU

We are living in the age of self-branding. What is a blog if not a self-branded entity? It is simply you, or me, or anyone, branded. It is someone deciding that they have something valuable to say to everyone else in the world, and the blog becomes their platform, pulpit and web-enabled megaphone — their brand.

I am convinced that Facebook is actually the death knell to self-branding. I know this is counter-intuitive, but just hear me out. Facebook masquerades as self-branding, but if you treat your Facebook page like most people do – posting everything from your most random, scattered thoughts to your deepest, most profound soliloquies – you are actually watering down your "brand" so much as to make it meaningless. In essence, you are "unbranding" yourself. Imagine all the potential brands that are floating around in the muck of Facebook ("Facemuck?"), waiting to be coalesced into a common theme and broadcast to the rest of the world. Today, those potential Pulitzer Prize-winning narratives go no further than the lucky souls who happen to be on your friends list. No offense, but what a waste.

Channel this material into a brand (a la a blog), and you get instant marketing power, a platform, a message that is heard by the rest of the world. The leverage creates new value, momentum and clarity, not to mention longevity and discoverability. Certainly, there are common themes and patterns in our Facebook posts – politics, religion, families, relationships, music, movies, etc. – that could be rounded up and combined into a well-defined "brand." What happens to all that stuff, otherwise? Does it get archived and preserved for future generations? Will our grandkids one day be staring at some glowing screen that displays our Facebook rants, status updates, notes and musings? Let's hope not.

Sadly, all that we pour into our Facebook pages and similar profiles is really going straight from our hearts to the worldwide trash can, or the trash "cloud," as it is now called. It has a shelf life shorter than sushi and evaporates as quickly as the spring rain. What a shame. And we thought that little note we posted the other day was going to change the world.

If the world had only known…

_____QUESTIONS TO CONSIDER_____

- Is there a common thread running through many of your Facebook posts? Do you tend to emphasize politics, religion, sports, business, family, etc.?
- Have you ever stepped back and marveled at the value and richness that lurks within your "statuses?"
- Are there any words of wisdom, memories, photos, etc., that you want to pass on to future generations? Wouldn't it be a waste if they never saw an inkling of them?

NEXT STEPS

- Identify at least one potential "brand" in your Facebook posts, photos and notes.
- Give it a name.
- Create a separate blog around this them to reach people you don't already know.
- Consider other ways to capture your profound thoughts and memories that will be more accessible and personal.

-12-
THE TWISTED VALUE OF THE "GREEN" BOTTLECAP

In the 1986 film *The Color of Money*, the characters played by Hollywood superstars Paul Newman and Tom Cruise make a fortune as pool-hustlers. They eventually square off against one another in the movie's final conflict, where each character shows his true color (so to speak). The movie grossed nearly $77 million in box office sales and rentals, greatly eclipsing its budget of only $13.8 million, according to Wikipedia. Obviously, the movie lived up to its name: it brought in a lot of "green" – the color of money.

Fast forward to the present. "Green" now symbolizes a global movement, a progressive culture, an enlightened lifestyle. Today, you're "green" when you use less energy, emit fewer pollutants, recycle everything, tap everything from solar power to surf winds and ride your kid's scooter to work. Accomplish all this, and your Earth-loving neighbors will be green with envy.

The same goes for business, where "green" is the most popular color nowadays. Going "green" can save you a lot of "green," earn you a lot of "green," and even though it can cost you a whole Crayola factory full of "green" to be "green," it can also put you solidly in the "black" if you play your cards right. Proudly displaying your "green-ness" can earn you all the public relations points you'll ever need with a buying public so soaked in "green" that it looks like a clover colony.

So as noble as it sounds to be "green," once again, it's still all about money. For business, anyway.

And so, a society blinded by the glow, glory and glamour of "green" – like Cruise's character in The Color of Money – tends to overlook any potential fallout from the rampant reductionism and idealistic idolatry that now characterize the ethos of "eco."

Case in point: Poland Spring bottled water.

Poland Spring's water bottles are sporting a new cap. We're supposed to be excited about this. Here's the marketing text from the label – no doubt scribed and polished by Nestle's multimillion dollar marketing department:

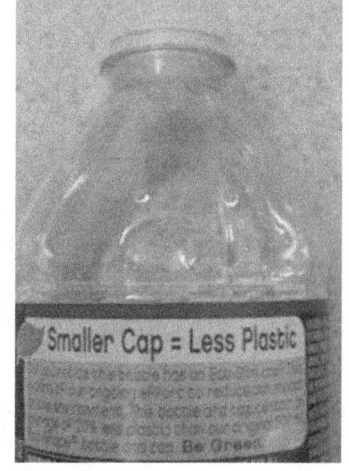

"Smaller cap = Less Plastic. Did you notice this bottle has an Eco-Slim cap? This is part of our ongoing effort to reduce our impact on the environment. This bottle and cap contain an average of 20% less plastic than our original 500 ml Eco-Shape bottle and cap. Be Green."

The cap is definitely smaller and thinner than its predecessor. It is rather small and slight. It also twists off more quickly, meaning you tend to drop it more easily. The bottle itself is thinner, as well, so be careful when you open a fresh one. If you squeeze it too hard, the water will spurt out all over you. Overall, the product just feels cheap in your hands (but of course, we're still paying the same price).

So there you have it. "Green" is better. Even if it's worse.

Upon further examination, it's actually much worse.

Read on ... (from the label):

"WARNING: Cap is a small part and poses a CHOKING HAZARD, particularly for children."

Did you notice anything sick about this? Put it all together and it sounds like: "It's okay to risk your child's life because we're saving the environment." Now, who in their right mind would make that deal?

Apparently, a lot of people would. According to the Nestle web site, Poland Spring is "one of the most popular bottled water brands in the northeast USA." We're swallowing their sales pitch right along with their water.

But we're also swallowing a few caps. Bottled water caps pose a very real choking hazard, as illustrated by the death of a 7-year-old girl a few years ago. In fact, health advocacy group livestrong.com lists bottle caps as one of the top 10 choking risks for children.

Have our values become so twisted that we're willing to sacrifice a life for the sake of a little "green" PR and a healthier bottom line? If they have, God help us all. We are trading a theoretical and negligible benefit for the very real horror of a choking child. All in the name of money. Code word: "green."

Now we know why the Bible tells us that "the love of money is the root of all evil." (I Timothy 6:10).

As you know, I'm all about reducing waste and delivering value while expending the least amount of energy and effort.

But there's a limit to that. When it risks the safety of our customer – or anyone, for that matter – we've crossed the line. It's time for Nestle to step back.

I'm sure there's a way to be "green" without imperiling a defenseless child. Hopefully, Nestle's engineers will apply their ingenuity to that end ... and give their marketers something truly noble to trumpet about.

QUESTIONS TO CONSIDER

- Did Poland Spring intend to devalue the life of a child by reducing the size of the cap?
- Can you think other instances where pursuit of a noble cause actually had detrimental, unintended consequences?
- How far should companies go to save money and/or the environment?

NEXT STEPS

- Reflect upon your own values. Are there any areas where you've "gone too far" in pursuit of what seemed like a noble cause?
- If you lead a business team, review your corporate values. Compare these to your policies and practices. Note any discrepancies or inconsistencies.
- Ensure your team knows the boundaries that should not be crossed in pursuit of a corporate mission.

-13-
WATERY WORKAROUND: WASTE-BUSTER OR WASTE-MAKER?

In a previous blog entry, I wrote about the workaround I created to deal with a leaky shower faucet. Rather than fix the real problem – worn out seals on the cold water side – I created a nifty workaround to capture the dripping water and transfer it to a nearby toilet tank after the occasional flush.

The system of stewardship I created was the result of much thought, study, innovation and industriousness. Today, I am proud to say, it has taken on a life of its own. Not just a temporary fix, it has become quite an elaborate process, complete with its own set of rules, tools and procedures, and has become a permanent part of our daily routine.

With this workaround, I not only displayed a penchant for process, but I achieved an even nobler goal: I have saved an estimated 1,000 gallons of water!

But being a hero hasn't been easy. Here are just a few of the issues I've addressed as I've worked to perfect this clever workaround:

When we first started, a mop pail was sufficient to capture a day's drips. Over time, the drip worsened and sometimes the pail overflowed before it could be emptied. To compensate, I began emptying the pail more often. This might sound like more of a chore than a rewarding waste-buster, but I know it's for a good cause and that keeps me going.

I don't know how you handle this at your house, but at ours, we don't flush with every use ("if it's yellow, let it mellow," as they say). With all this extra water lying around, we've started flushing more. Otherwise, the pail will overflow and we'll waste the excess. Can't have that! While this may feel counterintuitive (aren't we just trading water down one drain for water down the other?), we've chosen to ignore that. The goal is to save that dripping water and use it somehow. We have to accomplish that goal, come (that really hot place) or high water, so to speak. So, we've adjusted our flushing patterns to keep up with the escalating waste.

The workaround system requires regular attention. What if we are gone all day and the pail doesn't get emptied? Maybe we can hire a neighbor to empty the pail while we are gone? This seems a little overboard, not to mention embarrassing. So on those days, the extra drips go down the drain. We'll just to have live with that until someone volunteers to toilet-sit.

Lately, the drip has gotten so bad we've had to upgrade the catch mechanism to a 5-gallon bucket. This takes all day to fill, requiring only one emptying per day (usually in the a.m.). Unfortunately, due to its weight, I have to do the emptying.

A full bucket is downright heavy. I have to be careful not to spill the water. It has happened a few times, to my chagrin. I keep an extra towel handy just in case. I also try to wait until the very last second to life the bucket and re-fill the tank, so I don't have to hold the heavy bucket for too long.

Sometimes I do forget to replace the bucket. I hate it when

I do that. It's really frustrating to realize a whole day's drips have been lost! When this happens, I take a moment to stare at the sparkling drops of wasted water on the floor of the shower, pondering what could have been. This moment of self-chastisement motivates me to do better.

Other times, I flush and forget to grab the bucket. What a waste! I guess nobody's perfect.

Now, I'm not sure what I'll do if the *toilet tank* starts leaking… Guess I'll cross that bridge when I come to it.

If you're impressed and want to implement a similar system, below is a basic workflow diagram to get you started:

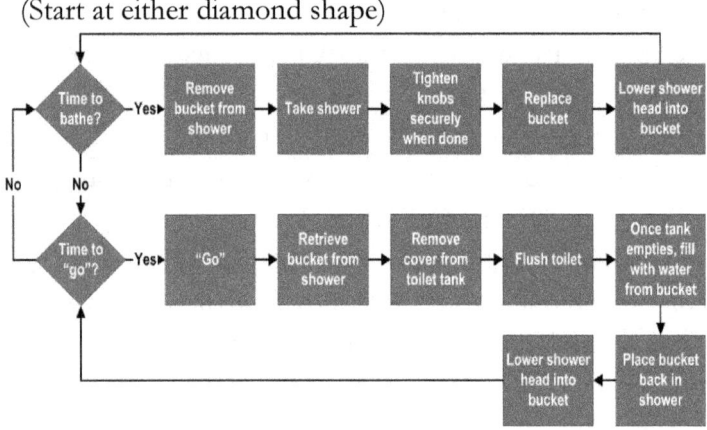

I'm also available for consultation as you develop your own system. Just remember: I'm a process engineer, not a plumbing engineer.

Finally, as you see waste around you at home or at work, don't let that waste go down the drain. Build your workaround today and be a good steward!

QUESTIONS TO CONSIDER

- Have you built similar workarounds?
- Did this workaround achieve the ideal state, or was it still elusive? (hint: think, "no drips")
- What types of waste did the workaround actually create?
- What leads to workarounds? Laziness? Lack of understanding the problem? Lack of money?

NEXT STEPS

- Ask your team or group to list all the different workarounds that they currently use.
- Prioritize the list by time in use, time required to complete, complexity, ineffectiveness or other factors.
- Commit to eliminating the top workaround this month by pursuing a solution for the underlying problem.

-14-
SYSTEMS THINKING HELPS TO SANITIZE THE "WASTE"

McDonald's recently tore down one of its first restaurants in our area and replaced it with a brand new, hip and stylish eatery. The layout and furnishings are sleek and clean, there are flat-screen TV's strategically located throughout the dining area and a convenient wi-fi network so you can surf while you scarf. (I'm not really sure if the menu is new; I pretty much stick with the $1 value offerings. Cheap but filling.)

The progressive design flows all the way to the restrooms, where the latest sanitation systems are on display. The urinals are touchless; just step away, and away it goes. The sinks are also touchless; just place your hands underneath the faucet, and a perfect amount of water automatically cascades down onto your hands. Drying your hands is a sanitary cinch – just wave your hands underneath a powerful wall-mounted dryer, and you're done in seconds.

Reinforcing this emphasis on sanitation is a comforting sign that reads, "Employees Must Wash Hands."

While that's certainly a warm-fuzzy, there's just one

problem: employees could wash their hands all afternoon, but they wouldn't be clean when they got back to the grill. They have to grab the door handle to get out. Imagine if the previous guy didn't even stop by the sink on the way out – an employee would pick up all his germs (and more) when he grabs that handle. And he'd carry it all the way back to the grill or register and pass it along to everyone he serves.

Yuck. Make that "McYuck." McGerm-X anyone?

There are actually several lessons in systems thinking here:

- This marvelous system of sanitation collapses because the design was not thought-through all the way to the end. Individual components may have been optimized, but the effectiveness of the overall system was overlooked. As a result, the system failed to meet the goal. So much for all those great fixtures.
- Technology (in this case, fancy fixtures) alone doesn't guarantee a certain result. It may be fun to install the latest toys, but an effective process is a lot more fun – especially for the customer.
- This also points to the power of the value stream for the customer. Every point along the way should be designed to add value. Missing the mark at one step can ruin the whole experience.

Inevitably, we find workarounds to compensate for badly designed systems. In this case, my workaround was my sleeve. I'd much rather have had a swinging door. And then, maybe a small fry. To go, of course. And cooked by somebody who has never used the restroom.

_____QUESTIONS TO CONSIDER_____

- Who stands to benefit more from McDonald's' restroom

upgrade? The restaurant or the patron?
- What are some underlying reasons the overall system was overlooked in favor of individual upgrades?

NEXT STEPS

- Consider technology upgrades that are made at your company. Are they made with single-step improvements in mind or entire system efficiencies? Do budgetary constraints play a role?
- Take note of other upgrades/improvements companies make that are touted as being consumer- or eco-friendly. From a broad perspective, are they better for the consumer, the company or both?
- The next time your team or department is considering an upgrade to facilities or technology, predict the impact on overall processes, systems and flow. Strive for a solution that meets everyone's goals – including the customers'.

-15-
VARIETY: THE SPICE OF STRIFE

You've all heard the saying, "Variety is the spice of life." There are many areas of life where variety is essential to prevent boredom and ensure individuality. For example, clothes – who wants to have nothing but white shirts in their closet? And cars – can you imagine a world filled with nothing but 4-door Mercedeses? (Their value would plummet and every hit-and-run accident would involve a vehicle with the same description.) How about shoes? If all we had were flip-flops – which I hate, by the way – I'd be barefoot every day of the week and wouldn't be able to go into a single gas station or grocery store. Everybody else would have a single tan line from toe-to-ankle and a profound crease between the first two toes.

As you can see, variety can be healthy in some ways.

But it can also be unhealthy. For example, have you tried to order anything at McDonald's lately? It could take a year to read all the different choices, combinations and prices. Eventually, you just give up and order a Big Mac and fries to escape the information overload. And as tasty as that is, it certainly isn't healthy.

This reminds me of the time my mother, my little sister and I walked into the "63 Flavors" ice cream parlor circa 1980. They had every combination and flavor you could think of at the time, yet my sister ordered – you guessed – vanilla. I burst out laughing. "They've got 63 flavors and you want 'vanilla?'" I exclaimed. "What's the matter with you?"

When I look back on it, I realize she wasn't the one with the problem. She had simply been given way too many choices. To simplify and keep from going into panic mode, she just went with vanilla. She knew what that would taste like, at least. So she succeeded in making a puzzling and perilous situation predictable.

In our effort to offer everything to everybody, I fear that we are losing our ability to give one thing to one person. We're making the transaction too cumbersome and confusing. We're overwhelming our customers with variety – giving them a dash of everything from the spice rack, instead of just a teaspoon of salt and pepper, or seasoning to taste, or not at all.

I truly believe this phenomenon is out of control. Have you tried shopping for shoes lately? Even in a modest shoe department, there is a mind-numbing array of sizes and styles. How can you decide which is best? There's always another one on the shelf to try on. Do you keep a scorecard to narrow your choices based on certain selection criteria – color, shape, comfort, price, brand, versatility, durability, etc., etc., etc.? (Trust me, there are probably some geeks out there who do this. Embarrassingly, my wife wishes I would adopt this approach, as she now refuses to go shoe-shopping with me. Last time, she locked herself in the ladies room so she wouldn't kill me.)

So, what is the lesson for us as professionals? Simply this:

simplify. If at all possible, do one thing, and do it well. Put yourself in your customers' shoes – would you know what to order if you walked up to your own menu on the wall? If not: slash and burn. Use pictures instead of words. Consolidate. Aggregate. Eliminate. Let people breathe, for goodness' sake.

And remember, just because you can, doesn't mean you should. Show some restraint, and put some time back into your customers' day. Hold off on the spice, and watch their blood pressures go down, while your sales go up.

QUESTIONS TO CONSIDER

- Have you ever been overwhelmed by too many choices?
- How did you respond?
- What types of waste could be linked to unnecessary variety or complexity?

NEXT STEPS

- Examine your life and your workspace.
- Identify areas where "choice" is out of control. It might be in your clothes closet or supply closet.
- Begin eliminating the extra, unnecessary choices and standardizing to the essential and best.
- Repeat this process at least 3-4 times per year.

-16-
SIGNS OF WASTE

Greetings, fellow waste-busters!

I want to highlight a phenomenon we are all familiar with: the ridiculous road sign. You know, the ones that probably repel more business than they attract.

Here is a classic example from my hometown:

Try reading that one out loud. This sign was left like this for months. Obviously, the business didn't care. Everybody went about their work lives as if there was nothing unusual outside on the marquee. Eventually, they just took everything down and the blank sign remained for several weeks ... until recently when they decided to run a "Super Bowl Special." Of course, that announcement still remains – at least most of it. Here's the new version, taken 10 days after the Super Bowl:

Yes, it's now become the ever-popular "Super Owl" special. Those who give a hoot can get it while it lasts, I guess.

I saw this example recently and couldn't resist sharing it:

I think I have the perfect ad campaign to go with the sign:

"For the best-looking lawn in town, call "Grass Cuting!"

Anyway...

Who knows — maybe the sign will actually work by inspiring calls from teachers and concerned spell-checkers all over town. They can barter spelling lessons for some great "grass cuting!"

Here's another example I noticed recently:

Looks like somebody came a few letters short of ... well ... words. So, what are we looking for on Facebook, again?

There are at least a few lessons to be learned in these humorous-but-tragic "signs of waste":

- If your letters won't stick to the sign, don't put them up there. Don't even get the ladder out.
- If you can't spell, take a dictionary with you. Better yet, have somebody else do it (who can spell).
- If you don't have enough letters to spell your message, don't mix and match with numbers or expect people to fill in the gaps. You're more likely to cause a crash as they focus on figuring out what your sign is supposed to say.
- Don't put up a sign and just forget about it. Hire a guy with stilts to fix it every day if you have to; don't just ignore it, or everyone else will, too (and they'll tell everyone else about it, and some waste-buster guy will write a blog about it).

Now, don't get me wrong. These are great local businesses with hard-working people and conscientious owners. The problem is the performance of the sign rarely lives up to its allure; it's never the beautiful attraction it's supposed to be. Too often, it makes you a laughing stock instead of a millionaire.

Perhaps the biggest hit is the damage to business reputation. Be honest: Would you be comfortable with either of these guys cooking your food? Didn't think so.

Got any "signs of waste" of your own to share? I'd love to see them. Send them to me and I'll add them to the mix.

_____QUESTIONS TO CONSIDER_____

- What is your reaction to a sign with errors, missing letters or outdated information?
- What is your impression of the business?
- Are you compelled to stop and buy, or simply point and laugh?
- What types of waste can result from such signs?

_____NEXT STEPS_____

- Talk to your team about the importance of accurate, clear and professional communications with customers.
- Emphasize that even simple mistakes, such as typos and grammatical errors, reflect poorly on the organization.
- Use the examples from this book to illustrate your point.
- Then, review your company's advertising and signage.
- Look for errors or omissions.
- Ensure communications are up-to-date.
- If you're "just too busy," ask someone else to do it.
- Repeat monthly or more often, if needed.

-17-
ONE LETTER CAN BE VERY IMPOTANT

Today I thought I'd start off with a visual…

Yes, you read that right: "We have eat pumps."

Now, this company must have known that people were going to do a double-take when they read this first sign, so they put up an identical sign on the other side of their parking lot that says the same thing:

"We have eat pumps."

I use this today as an illustration of how important a single letter can be. It can radically change the meaning of a word, or in this case, a sentence. Instead of making you rich, it can make you a laughing-stock. (My kids, in fact, laughed hysterically when they saw this sign. OK, I admit it — so did I.) You can't afford to get sloppy with your spelling, particularly if you're going to make an announcement to the world.

The same is true for your processes. You can't be too careful. You can't be too precise. You can't play "loosey-goosey" with how your work gets done. Every customer engagement is a chance to win, and a chance to fail. And every customer is important.

So I encourage you to sit with your people, document what they do, discuss it, evaluate it and continually improve it. Make sure the customer is at the center of everything that you do. Treat each customer engagement like it is precious. Cradle it and caress it. (This will work quite well if you're in pediatrics or massage therapy.) Deliver value every step of the way. Cut out anything redundant or unnecessary. Minimize hand-offs and chances for errors.

One error could have you eating your words, your hat, or … like these guys … a pump. Lots of iron, I suppose. At least there's that.

QUESTIONS TO CONSIDER

- Do you have clear understanding and documentation of all of your business processes?
- Have you assessed where these processes might fail, and taken steps to alleviate the risk, impact or frequency of failure?

NEXT STEPS

- If not, don't delay —meet with your team and document or map out your processes right away. At least review what you *think* you do.
- Discuss recent errors or failures that led to a complaint, return or downtime.
- Focus on identifying and correcting the root cause by asking "why did that happen" to get to the bottom of the issue.

-18-
DOES THIS GIVE YOU A WARM FUZZY?

Greetings, fellow Quality evangelists!

If you're like me, you did a double-take when you read this sign. And then you cringed. Let's think about this for a moment, shall we?

First, there's the ambiguity: "9 and up" – is that an age requirement? Certainly there are laws that would speak to that. But if not, I have 5 kids who will be filling out an application momentarily.

So let's err on the side of logic and assume that the "9" should be "$9." Is that any better? Managers – you know, people with advanced organizational, interpersonal and analytical skills – making $9 an hour? Now there's a company that's serious about running a tight ship. Only the best and brightest need apply. Particularly if they want to be the sign manager.

Here's the best news: This was posted outside a major restaurant franchise. Do you want someone making $9 an hour to be in charge of the people making your food? To be the one who puts together the sanitation plan to raise the health department grade from a "C-minus" to an "A?"

Me neither.

While I'm on the subject, here's another great example from a major chicken restaurant down the road:

What's in that box? Eight chickens that lay golden eggs? The Colonel's secret recipe? (Note: This is a competing chain.) Whatever it is, it better be good.

Must be something with the number 9; gets the sign-boy all confused when he's on that ladder. "Is this a '6' or a '9?' I can never tell. Aw, man … what was this supposed to say? I guess that's close enough."

All of this angst is predicated on the fact that signs should say something about the inside of a business. They should reflect the inner being, the best there is to offer, the reason to come inside. Are the people detail-oriented? Customer-focused? Quality-aware? Older than 9 and making more than $9 an hour?

Unfortunately, sloppy signs like these taint one's perception of the inner workings of the business – doubly not good when it's a restaurant. Might even cause one to think twice before pulling in for a bite. The first sign might attract hundreds of potential applicants, but drive away the patrons the low-dollar managers would serve.

The one below ... well ... it will just make you sad:

So close, and yet so far.

I suppose I can overlook some things – a missed decimal point; a typo here and there; a dropped letter; a "5" that doubles as an "S" – unless it's a tutoring business, of course.

Or a sign shop. Everybody else gets a pass. That is, until there's a hair in my salad. Then I'm history ... after I voice my concerns to the $9 manager.

Later, Lean gator!

_____QUESTIONS TO CONSIDER_____

- Have you ever avoided a business because of its sign? Why?
- How do you think having an outdated or erroneous sign affects the mindset of the workers?

_____NEXT STEPS_____

- Express your concern to a local business whose sign has been errant for awhile.
- Note the reaction. This will provide great insight into the mindset of the company.

-19-
DOES THIS GIVE YOU A WARM FUZZY?
(PART OOOOH)

We've all seen them.

You know, those imposing signs that strike fear into the heart of every fast-food and convenience store employee in the USA: "Employees Must Wash Hands."

I wonder how many defiant workers have stuck their tongue out at those signs and marched their contaminated selves right back to their work stations. Why wouldn't they? What will happen? Bells and sirens will go off as soon as they touch the door handle? Infection control Ninjas will descend from the rafters, chop off their hands and expeditiously disinfect the premises? Obsessive-compulsive elves will materialize from out of nowhere, wipe them to death, check them, wipe them, check them and then wipe them again?

If only they would.

Do these signs have any effect whatsoever on the problem they're supposed to fix? Or are they just there so the local Health Department inspector can check that box and the store manager can brag about having a germ-free workplace?

You know the answer, but you're afraid to admit it, because you EAT at these places (as do I, but let's move on).

And why wouldn't the Health Department want EVERYBODY to wash their hands? Are the employees the nastiest and most contagious of all? Like they're not going to pick their nose or sneeze on the way back to the grill, just before making your bacon cheeseburger and tossed salad, anyway. Get real. And like the trucker in the next stall is just reading the comics. Come on!

Another observation: Why are these signs always NEXT TO THE MIRROR, where the only way the employees will see them is if they're ALREADY washing their hands? Hey – they're the good guys (or, more likely, gals)! It's the nasty sloths – most of whom can't read, anyway, but that's beside the point – that we're trying to force into compliance with our cowering signs!

Come to think of it, why do we have to tell people to wash their hands, anyway? Has anyone found a germ-free way to use the restroom yet? I'd be interested to know ... or maybe not.

Anyway, never mind these questions. Just check the box and call it a good process. Do your business, wash your hands, grab the door handle with the tip of your pinky and pray over your food.

Oh yeah, and don't forget the Germ-X.

See there, the signs are working, after all.

In-sanitation Grade: A.

_____QUESTIONS TO CONSIDER_____

- Do you think such signs are effective? What is the typical compliance rate?
- What would be a more effective way to ensure the cleanliness of employees?

_____NEXT STEPS_____

- Look for areas in your business (or home) where you are relying on a sign to control behavior.
- Determine the real compliance rate (either by observed measure or estimation).
- Interview the intended audience. Do they notice the sign? Do they comply? Why or why not? What would improve their compliance?

-20-
THE FUEL-PUMP SIGN PARADE

Here's what I want to know:

If all of these warnings and announcements are so deathly important, then why are they thrown up here in such a way that you can't read any of them? Which one do you pay attention to first?

- The one that says "warning?"(top left)
- The one that says "notice?"
- The one that says "please?" (Mommy would have liked that one)

- What about the red ones vs. the yellow ones vs. the white ones vs. the black ones?
- Or the all-caps vs. the first-letter caps vs. the tall compressed caps vs. the small spread-out caps?
- Triangles or other arresting shapes vs. official seals and certifications?
- Full sentences vs. phrases?
- Ones that light up?
- How about the ones with logos or pictures? Those are usually easy to digest. My 4-year-old knows every restaurant in the world by its logo, and she can't even read yet.
- What about the ones with the biggest letters – for example, "PAY AT PUMP?" Well, at least they have their priorities straight. Next priority should be to hire a graphic designer who can instill some order into this chaos, before somebody does something rash ... like put their card in upside down. Can't they read?

Don't be surprised to find some guy talking on his cell phone and smoking a cigarette while pumping fuel into a gas can on the back of his pickup truck with his engine running. Forgive him if he doesn't see the signs telling him that each of these things is a bad idea. There are so many messages up there, you just can't look at them. ANY of them. You don't WANT to look at them. It's a sign barrage! It hurts your head, assaults your eyes, to look at them. It's like looking at the sun. Even if you want to, you can't do it.

This is sight pollution! There's no rhyme or reason to how they're arranged, sized, designed, positioned or mounted. But if you miss one, you're up in smoke. Literally. And the system crashes and burns because of it.

So what do you do during that 5-7 minute span while you're lazily pumping gas into your vehicle's parched repository? That's right – you stare at the electronic digits as they spiral toward an ungodly amount that reminds you the kids will need an alternative to college. You are hypnotized by the blur of the digits as they race indiscernibly toward their final destination. You're drooling. Your zipper is down and you don't even know it. Your socks don't match. Your shoe is untied. Your seat belt is closed in your door. Your left blinker is still on. Your next-door neighbor or pastor is pumping gas directly across from you, but you are oblivious. And your gas cap rests dangerously on top of your car, sending out silent cries to not be forgotten. You try to anticipate when the cents digits will be close to that round number you're aiming at ... and then you let off suddenly, check the amount, and pulse and click your way to the hoped-for amount. Only to exceed it by .01, as usual.

But you don't look at those signs. They're yelling at you, but you're not hearing a thing. You're so close, but yet so far. You grab your receipt, jump back in the car, and drive away, focusing once again on the things that really matter as your mind emerges from its temporary hibernation. Lucky to be alive, since you broke every rule on the pump without even knowing it. Having cheated the gas-pump sign gods once again, you race down the highway a free spirit ... but only until you get to restaurant row or the commercial district or the airpark or the school district or traffic-calming zone or the nature conservancy or the historic district or the government buildings or the hospital region or the construction zone or the interstate interchange or billboard bonanza ... so that eventually, your mind longs for the dopamine of the fueling station, where it can once again stand still and let the slings and arrows of rules and regulations fly harmlessly past, in a sea of reds and yellows, as the dancing digits rock you to sleep amidst the chaos and cacophony that is the fuel-pump sign parade.

QUESTIONS TO CONSIDER

- Do you bombard your customers with instructions, rules or warnings?
- How are these directives delivered?
- Are all of the guidelines followed consistently? Or do staff find they have to regularly remind patrons of certain ones?

NEXT STEPS

- Study the reliability, placement and clarity of your rules, policies and guidelines.
- Seek input from the users. Are the directives communicated clearly and effectively? Which ones stand out? Which ones are overlooked?
- Strive for simplicity and clarity. Eliminate unnecessary rules or communications.
- Combine, aggregate or logically rearrange your signs – don't just make them fit in the available space.

-21-
THE SIGNS OF WASTE ARE EVERYWHERE

I started the "signs of waste" series mostly by accident. I noticed a few ridiculous signs in town that had not been updated in, well, forever, and consequently they were advertising things that no longer made any sense ("fall bike sale" in April). Then, I noticed a few more. Pretty soon, they were all over town. It's kind of like when you buy a new car, you suddenly notice all the other cars on the road that are just like yours. They were there all along, but you weren't tuned in. Now it's like everybody has one!

Apparently, everybody in my town wants a sign that makes you scratch your head or laugh out loud. If that were truly the intent, it wouldn't be a big deal. But in these cases, what are supposed to be serious, informative signs, instead are only entertaining distractions. Their intended messages are lost and the attempt at communication fails. Hence the name, "signs of waste." And I am compelled to fight waste by making an example of these hilarities, so that you will think twice, proofread and dummy-proof any sign you ever think of displaying. Or else, you just might be featured in this illustrious gallery.

GO GET YOUR MUDA

Here are the latest additions to our illustrious collection:

Better drive slowly ... there are some large folks crossin'!

Don't break your neck reading this one...

I disagree. In absolutely no circumstances should you accept pp i a o !

Say what?

Best stylst in town, they say. (Only one, but still the best.)

And my personal favorite:

There has got to be a better way to spend $35 than on wasteful vanity.

_____QUESTIONS TO CONSIDER_____

- Why are there so many "signs of waste?"
- How does this compare with your own experience?

NEXT STEPS

- Pay attention to the "signs of waste" you notice around your own town. Consider making your own collection.
- If you use signs, design a process to ensure they are clear and kept up-to-date. Let others read and interpret them before they are implemented. Assign responsibility for regular review and set a maintenance schedule.
- And when you advertise a promotion on a sign, take steps to measure the response and effectiveness. This will reinforce the importance of clear, current and correct communications.

-22-
LEAN TIMES CALL FOR LEAN MEASURES

In these lean economic times, when businesses cannot simply:
- hire more people
- buy more machines
- expand their facilities, or
- install new software,

how can they possibly:
- increase productivity
- improve quality
- be more competitive, and
- keep up with demand?

The only answer is:
- By improving their processes.

You know, with the economy the way that it is, you'd think that people would be knocking down my door to get help. So, why do I have to go to them?

Admit it: process improvement sounds boring. There's no real excitement there. We're just changing what we're doing; how fun can that be? We'd rather stay the same and just "grin and bear it."

It gets fun when you connect what you're doing to what you make, what you provide and who you are. Every result is the birth-child of a process, just like a baby is the result of ... well, you know what causes that, don't you?

It gets exciting when you realize you can radically transform a business – indeed, the very lives that it touches – with process improvement. And you can do it continually, methodically, routinely, simply. No fancy gadgets or long list of capital letters after your name is required.

But it will require something of you – you will have to talk to people. Better yet, you will have to listen. You will have to admit things could actually be better ... and then commit to making them so. Maybe that's the part we don't like. The time, self-reflection and energy required. It's easier just to continue on and hope for the best. Maybe the next customer to come in the door will have standards that match ours, we hope. (Fat chance.)

Customers don't wait for us to change. If our standards don't meet theirs, they expect us to adjust, or they'll just find a better partner. It's time we acted like we cared, stopped taking people for granted. The best way to show you care is to change. Now do it. Or do you prefer lean sales?

_____QUESTIONS TO CONSIDER_____

- How often do you engage in a formal process review and improvement effort?
- Is this a routine, standardized practice?

- How do you normally make improvements? Do you rely upon effort or technology?
- Do you hire more people, or just tell the ones you have to work longer/harder, to be more productive?

_____NEXT STEPS_____

- Seriously consider adopting a standardized improvement framework, such as Lean Six Sigma or other similar methodologies.
- Take a Lean Six Sigma class to build your understanding (any level).
- Start teaching the principles (such as those found in this book) to others and really applying them to your everyday work.
- Begin with identifying your customers' needs and values and connecting them to your processes (the things that you do to give customers what they want).
- Measure your current success in meeting your customers' needs. Where do you fall short? Where do you excel?
- Dedicate yourself to continuous improvement using your new improvement methodology.
- Be patient. Crawl, walk, run – in that order.

-23-
THE VALUE OF CHANGE

Sometimes you learn more from your defeats than from your victories.

Here's one example.

I recently made a proposal to do some work for a government client. I was glad to make the proposal, as I had spent at least 44 hours of my time marketing to and meeting with their leaders.

After so much time spent with them, I was certain I had the job.

And then things took a turn.

They worried. They worried about my learning curve. They worried about justifying the expense. They worried about backlash from their staff.

The bottom line is – they worried. Instead of seeing the potential, they worried about the fallout. Instead of focusing on the VALUE of change, they worried about the PRICE. In the process, they underestimated the COST of staying the same.

So here's what I learned: I can't make anyone want to change. That has to come from within.

Even when it comes to the government.

Never underestimate the value of change, or the cost of staying the same. Properly evaluated, both factors should create a burning platform from which anyone would want to leap head-long into the future.

_____QUESTIONS TO CONSIDER_____

- Are you open to change?
- Really? (ask others)
- When was the last time you mad a meaningful, intentional change to one of your processes?
- When someone suggests a change, do you explore the idea readily, or resist skeptically?

_____NEXT STEPS_____

- Make a list of three things you know need to change, based on feedback, experience or intuition.
- Make a plan to address each of them, one at a time.
- Announce your intention to change to others. Recruit accountability partners.
- Encourage others to do the same.

-24-
WHAT YOUR PROCESS SAYS ABOUT YOU

You market. You advertise. You brand yourself.

You dress nicely. You make eye contact. You smile.

You say, "Have a nice day;" "Thanks for your business;" and "Referrals are always welcome."

You give suckers to your bank customers, refrigerator magnets to your home-buyers and calendars to your insurance clients.

But nothing you do says more to your customers than a process that either sets them free or holds them hostage. Why? Because people value their time. They don't appreciate it when you waste it. To them, this feels inconsiderate, uncompassionate and careless.

Nowhere is this conflict between intention and perception more true than in healthcare. Day after day, nurses, receptionists, technologists, LPN's, aides, nurse practitioners and physicians pour their hearts and souls into their work, giving everything they have to improve someone else's quality of life. They skip meals, sacrifice sleep and personal health, toil away at all hours (almost dangerously so) and continually cram their brains with the latest research. And what they're saying through all of this is that they care deeply about their patients.

Are the patients getting this message? Maybe; but, chances are it's being drowned out by the inevitable wait times, excessive movement, paperwork and redundancies that still characterize most doctor's appointments.

In many medical offices, patients show up anticipating a 15-30-minute commitment, but what they often find is that their *wait* is at least this much. Then, an hour or more later, they are exacerbated as they finally walk out the door. Along the way, they've visited multiple stations to be signed in, registered, weighed, examined, billed and dispositioned. Imagine what a patient might be thinking: here's a system that takes advantage of me and treats me like a second-class citizen ... because once I'm here, I'm here.

But this perception could not be any further from the truth. No one in healthcare looks down on anyone who comes through the door. The people working in medical offices are not there just for the money, and they're certainly not there to waste anybody's time; they come in and sweat bullets each day because they love what they do and the people for whom they do it. But their actions, i.e. their processes, speak more loudly than their intentions, and their words. At the end of the day, customer service is not what you say, it's what you do and how you do it.

How are you treating your customers? Better yet, how are you "processing" your customers? Take an honest look, and then examine if your words and your processes are in agreement. If not, work on your processes. Your customers will hear you, loud and clear.

QUESTIONS TO CONSIDER

- Does the process your customer experiences reflect your commitment to customer service?
- What parts of it do customers have to "tolerate" in order to do business with you?
- Where do people wait? What do they complain about?
- Would *you* do business with you?

NEXT STEPS

- Open your suggestion box or complaint log. Read with an open mind what people are saying.
- Observe the customer experience. Be the customer yourself, if it helps.
- Interview patrons. Ask their opinions.
- Measure how well your process meets your commitments to service. How long do people wait? How often are orders remade? Which ones?
- Identify the processes and steps that are the culprits – not simply the people.

-25-
STANDARDIZE? ARE YOU CRAZY?

Today, I would like to redefine insanity.

I'm sure you have all heard the common definition of insanity: "Doing the same thing over and over again, but expecting (all together now) ... different results."

I submit to you that the inverse is also just as crazy, if not more so:

"Doing different things over and over again, but expecting the results to be the same." Now that's insane. How can that happen? Right – it can't!

As crazy as it sounds, this happens in business every day. In fact, it's the way most businesses are run. There really is little effort to standardize. Why? First of all, who has time? You have to get everybody together, talk it over, maybe draw it out (process map), reach a consensus – a daunting set of tasks for many companies. Plus, professionals have a visceral reaction to the thought of standardization. "It's boring; it's demeaning; it's intrusive. Nobody's gonna tell me how to do my job," they say (you know who you are).

As a result, many businesses just leave the results to chance, hoping they will all come out right somehow. Or, if they don't, maybe nobody will notice. (Trust me, the best businesses don't leave the results to chance. They *standardize*, because it minimizes decision-making and the risk of error.)

So, people do things differently, and customers feel the difference. But unless somebody complains really loudly, nothing gets done about it.

Your customers – and your employees – deserve better. They come to you for a good experience, and they expect it every time. If they don't get it, they will likely go elsewhere. Why? 'Cause they're not crazy! They're not going to waste their time while you figure things out. Think about it: Why do you frequent your favorite restaurant? Undoubtedly, a consistent experience is high on the list. That's why McDonald's has served billions of burgers. Kids and parents alike know what they're getting, whether it's in Atlanta, Georgia, or the former Soviet republic of Georgia. And for a parent, predictability rules.

So, if there are any areas of your business that you're unsure about, don't delay – standardize today. And always ask if they want fries with that.

_____QUESTIONS TO CONSIDER_____

- Why is standardization important to quality, consistency, service and sales?
- Is there any resistance to standardization in your business? Is so, why?
- Reflect on the last bad experience you had with a local company. Was that a typical experience? Why did it stand out?

NEXT STEPS

- Identify one critical area in your business that is essential to customer satisfaction or safety.
- Gather your team. Discuss the different ways work is done in that area.
- Seek to standardize to the safest, highest quality method.
- Set a plan to review the team's experience with this process regularly, and update as needed.

-26-
LATHER, RINSE, REPEAT ... OR DIE

For this edition, I would like to focus on a critical element to any successful business – the repeatable process.

First, let me share a frustrating, but humorous, illustration from my own life.

How many of you do your own cooking? Great ... I happen to NOT do much of my own cooking (except for breakfast and lunch, but those are easy). My wife does the heavy lifting in this department. And she's not just cooking for me. She's cooking for a small army of folks – for me, herself and the 6 kids who still live at home with us.

When we were first married, my wife had a few challenges in the kitchen. She would cook hamburgers that looked more like charcoal briquettes or hockey pucks. I think I broke a few front teeth in the first few years of marriage. My friends started calling me Alfred E. Neuman.

Thankfully, she got better, and today, she has several dishes that she cooks regularly and she receives regular compliments from her patrons. It's been at least a decade since I broke a bone in my mouth.

Every now and then, she'll make something exceptional –

teriyaki burgers or oriental fajitas, for example – and I'll be really impressed. I'll ask her how she made it. You can imagine my surprise when she says, "I don't know."

"What?" I'll exclaim. "How can you not know?"

"I mean, 'I don't know,'" she'll reply. "I don't ever measure anything, and I'm not even sure what spices I used. I just throw a little of this and a little of that in there, and hope it comes out right."

Thankfully, more often than not, it does. If it didn't, I'd be having breakfast twice a day.

But here's the point (and don't tell her I said this): Wouldn't it be better if she paid attention to what she was doing? Shouldn't she write something down so she can do it again the next time? That sure would make me feel a little better.

But that's not her way. Here's her reasoning:

"My mama never used recipes. She just tasted it to see if it was any good. If it was, she just stopped adding stuff."

OK, that may work for country kitchens, but is that good enough for business?

Hopefully not.

The only thing good enough for business is a repeatable process. In fact, I often say a business is nothing more than a repeatable process with repeatable sales.

The best example of this is the franchise. It takes a successful business model, standardizes it, and repeats it all over the country. This guarantees a similar experience no matter which one you happen to go into. And as the franchise owner, all you do is essentially follow the recipe.

Whether our businesses are large or small – franchisable or not – we should run them the same way – with a framework for every facet and function.

GO GET YOUR MUDA

Repeatable processes have several benefits for business. They:
- Can be defined and, therefore, improved
- Eliminate guesswork, uncertainty and variation
- Tend to be simpler and less complex
- Are transferable to new staff members
- Allow your employees to focus more on "delighters," rather than relearning the essentials
- Provide a consistent customer experience, and
- Give your business a personality, a culture, an identity

Now, what are the business processes that you can make repeatable?
- Sales prospecting
- Order-taking
- Product assembly
- Customer communications
- Billing
- Paying your taxes
- Trash disposal
- Supply-ordering
- Installation
- Repairs or service calls
- Time and activity tracking
- Complaints
- Rewards and recognition
- Process improvement

I like that last one the best.

I'm sure you get the point. Anything that you do repeatedly needs to be repeatable. That is, unless you like to invent a new way every time you do it. But that is incredibly tiring and time-consuming. As I like to say, "go with the flow" is not a repeatable process ... unless you're a piece of driftwood.

Instead, build repeatable processes and watch the repeat business beat a path to your door.

_____QUESTIONS TO CONSIDER_____

- Do you have standardized, repeatable processes to serve all of your customer categories?
- Do your employees comment about how simple and consistent their work is, or how complicated and variable?

_____NEXT STEPS_____

- Ask your employees or co-workers to identify specific challenges, complexities or gaps in their daily work.
- Ask them to complete the statement, "One thing I'm unsure about is _____."
- Tally and aggregate the results.
- Seek to clarify, simplify and fill these gaps, one by one.

-27-
7 STEPS FOR A BETTER BURGER

Greetings, fellow process geeks!

Yes, you know who you are. And the rest of us can tell by your blushing. So come on out. Show your face. Get a tan, for goodness' sake. Be proud of your process geek-dom!

There ... that's better.

Besides, you'll love this entry. It elaborates on a topic that makes all of our hearts go pit-a-pat. No, it's not burgers. That was just a teaser. It's the repeatable process!

Now simmer down. Don't overheat your laptops. And please hold your questions until the end – and your breath, if you have to.

The repeatable process is the foundation of business. Honestly, without it, you don't really have a business. You have a stream-of-consciousness exercise that frustrates your customers and employees alike. You have an identity crisis coupled with a case of capriciousness compounded by indecision and fraught with forgetfulness. And you have the nerve to call it artistic license.

Well, it's time to grow up, build a mature business and develop some consistency. Believe it or not, it won't be boring – it will be liberating, as it will finally give you real license to add sweetening flavors to your services that were never there before. That extra brush stroke; that extra seasoning; that extra perk your customers didn't expect. That's when life gets interesting.

I know what you're wondering: "This sounds great, but how do we build a repeatable process?"

And you call yourselves geeks. Nevertheless, I'm glad you asked. Now I can finally get to the point.

In the spirit of the repeatable process, here's a 7-step recipe you can use to create ... a repeatable process:

1. Get your people together – the ones who actually do the process, as well as others upstream and downstream of the process you're building. Ask them to map out the work they do – actually write down the steps, on a flip chart or something broadly visible is best. On Post-it notes is helpful, to allow for shuffling and revisions.
2. Once the map is built, have the team focus on these critical questions: What triggers the work? How do they decide who does the work? How does the work get handed off to the next department or function?
3. Iron out all these details; confirm with observation.
4. Document the process using the software of your choice – Visio, Powerpoint, etc.
5. Communicate the process to all. Allow for feedback, questions and revisions. Allow them team to actually own the process.
6. Identify the key metric for judging performance. Now, measure it – yield, volume, defect rate, cycle time, etc.

7. Review the process and its performance a month or so later – or whatever makes sense – and then do this regularly. Use data, voice of the associate and voice of the customer to indicate need for improvement. Make adjustments as necessary. Let the process map you've created be a living document.

You'll want to keep the following suggestions in mind as you build your process:

- It has to be feasible on a regular basis.
- It can't be so convoluted and complicated that no one can repeat it without consulting the user's manual or calling the help desk.
- It should rely on minimal hand-offs and delays. It should be built around flow.
- It should emphasize work that is valuable to the customer, not just easy for you.

Now, follow this recipe for the different areas of your business. It might even be best to start with a value stream map, which outlines the overall high-level flow of work, to identify your different functional areas. You can then follow this recipe for each of those areas.

By the way, my wife made a savory batch of teriyaki turkey burgers this past week – perfectly browned, wonderfully moist and melt-in-your-mouth good. That's the good news. Of course I asked her how she did it. All she knew is she put some teriyaki sauce in there, maybe a few other things, whatever was close-by. So the bad news is I may never have those burgers again – at least not those exact burgers. Maybe next time I should order a few-hundred of them and put them in our spare freezer. Then the only process she has to remember is to press the "Defrost" key on the microwave.

Uh-oh, gotta go … a frying pan is headed my way.

_____QUESTIONS TO CONSIDER_____

- Why do we allow complexity to filter into our work? Is it just natural? Can it be controlled, or is it inevitable?
- Does complexity tend to drive costs up, or down?
- How about quality? Timeliness? Service? Satisfaction? How are they affected?

_____NEXT STEPS_____

- Identify the most complex, confusing or confounding process in your work area or business.
- Commit to eliminating, or at least simplifying, one step in the process. (Simplification can mean fewer steps, fewer hand-offs or fewer people or tools required.)
- Once your team is comfortable in the new process, repeat.
- Continue repeating as long as necessary.
- For fun and encouragement, measure the impact of this simplification on timeliness, errors or satisfaction. Map out the trend over time.

-28-
HOW TO KEEP YOUR S-O-P MEETINGS FROM BEING A FLOP

Perhaps you've heard of the term "Standard Operating Procedures." It refers to the way everybody is supposed to do something. At least, that's the intention.

How do you think those procedures are developed? Usually, it's in 1 of 2 ways: 1) The boss said so. OR 2) The person doing the job said so. Generally, it's not a very customer-centered process.

These methods may at least get steps on paper, but for a process that involves more than 1 person (as most do), there is a better way: "the team says so."

This sounds easy, but it isn't. We all have had meetings where the team got together to decide what it was going to do. Everyone had his or her opinion. And everybody was right. Eventually, the meeting devolved into an argument. When it ended, each person was entrenched in their position. And nothing changed – except people were more reluctant to have any more meetings to discuss the process.

Net result: variation persisted, customers noticed and people kept complaining.

There is a simple cure to help prevent this fallout: process mapping. The team process-mapping method is the most effective way to minimize arguments and foster collaboration.

Central to this exercise is the process map itself. Without it, the conversation will ultimately spiral into another wrestling match, a battle of personalities, seniority, experience and wit. And so, the process map is the most essential tool for creating "SOP's."

Here's why:

- It makes the process under scrutiny visible and plain. It gives everybody something to look at simultaneously.
- It creates an objective reference point for discussion. People can stop arguing with each other and focus on the map – the process.
- It forces you to make decisions – do we do it this way, or that way? It helps you develop a standard way of doing things.

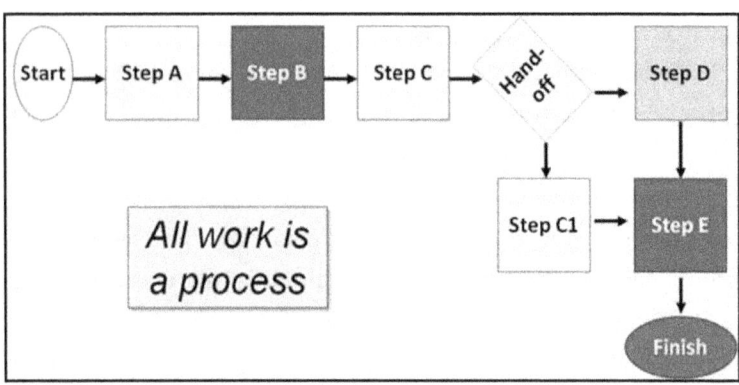

So the next time your team gets together to develop a standard, invite an artist – someone who can facilitate the group's drawing of a process map. It doesn't have to be perfect; it just needs to exist. Without it, you'll be talking in circles and getting nowhere.

One final thought – having a standard, even one that isn't perfect, is better than having multiple ways of doing the same thing. Unnecessary variation takes time, energy and memory and produces variable results (obviously). With a standard, you have a starting point for improvement. Without it, you have nothing to improve yet.

So grab those flip charts and markers. Use chisel tips instead of daggers. And make this a new standard for how you create your SOP's, OK?

OK!

QUESTIONS TO CONSIDER

- When things go wrong, does your team tend to blame the process, or a person? Why?
- If a person is blamed, what is usually the result? Is the team strengthened or weakened? More cohesive, or less?
- Does blaming, and even re-training, the person solve the problem?

NEXT STEPS

- Pick a troublesome process or function.
- Get your team together. Sketch out the workflow on a flip chart, or list steps on sticky notes and place in order.
- Identify problematic steps, the ones that tend to fail.
- Ask "why" these steps are problematic. Then ask "why" this first layer of causes occurs, then ask "why" those things occur … until you reach a point where the root

causes are revealed.
- Brainstorm fixes and simplifications for the root causes
- Try to minimize steps and hand-offs.
- Standardize to this new process, then repeat as needed to continually improve the standard.
- From now on, when things go wrong, go after the map – not the person.

-29-
(DON'T) PARDON THE INTERRUPTION

Today's rant is about distractions. So try to stay focused. (I will, too.)

Still there?

Good.

According to statistics, you won't be for long. Studies show that we get interrupted from our work 7 times per hour – about every 8-1/2 minutes or so. And once distracted, we may spend 25 minutes on that other thing (or things) before returning to our work.

Sound familiar? I bet it does. Our lives are filled with distractions – co-workers, phone calls, e-mails, UPS men, kids and spouses (for the telecommuters), loud airplanes, smartphone notifications, microwave beeps and dozens of other environmental intrusions. (As I write this from my home office, my daughter brings me today's mail – a monthly alumni magazine – and, of course, I thumb through it quickly to see what might be interesting. I just can't stop myself.)

Sure, there will always be unforeseen interruptions – like the dead battery in the wireless keyboard that is now forcing me to divert momentarily (if the text starts to lighten, you'll know why) – but the worst distractions are the ones we see all around us every day, right under our noses. When our minds wander, our eyes wander ... and then we're off to the races.

As I look around my own work area, I see the following items within arm's reach and eye-shot:

- Prospecting files
- Project files and related documents
- Junk mail
- Materials for a future blog
- My #1 business portfolio
- Books I'm reading
- My bill calendar
- Bill organizer and checkbooks
- Personal file cabinet
- Food and drink
- Memory joggers
- Stacks of filled up legal pads, waiting to be scoured for ideas and filed or discarded
- Receipts related to a recent home improvement project
- Post-it reminders in a somewhat neat little stack
- My value proposition board, which reminds me of why I'm in business, key messages, etc.
- Other nifty little things I'm working on – sales letters, tool ideas, process model diagrams (yes, I'm a process geek), etc.
- My laptop, for mobile productivity and my kids' playtime when they're in the office with me
- And, oh yes, my computer screen, with multiple browsers and documents open.

How can I possibly concentrate on one thing with all of those items around me, each one begging for attention? None of these is an interruption by nature, but I give each the power to be a distraction by bringing it into my circle of attention. If I really want to limit my distractions, I should clean up my work area, center on the priority, stratify the space, eliminate the clutter. I should make it possible to work on one thing at a time. My work area should look like one thing, not a million. Currently, anything can grab my attention, and often does.

Why is this so bad? Doesn't it inspire multi-tasking? Possibly, but who said multi-tasking was a good thing? (Don't believe the hype and overblown job descriptions.) And consider the meaning of the word "distraction": something that diverts you from your first priority. It diffuses your energy; splinters your focus; interrupts your flow; taxes your memory; slows you down; and leads to rework and errors. None of these is good.

Look around your desk or work area – how many different work items are in plain view and within easy reach? Does your work area reflect focused work or distracted work? Does it breed distractions? If so, why do you let this happen? Do a "5-why" on that and be honest with yourself (I'm doing one, myself). Your productivity may depend on it.

Gotta go. My 8-1/2 minutes are up. And so are yours.

_____QUESTIONS TO CONSIDER_____

- What are the things that tend to distract you from your top priority? List them out.
- Why do these items distract you? Why do they occur? Does your workspace breed interruptions? Do you secretly

foster distractions, but complain about them verbally?
- Address any hidden mindset you have that allows distractions to occur.
- Erect natural boundaries to distractions in your workspace.
- Take control of your work environment and attention span.

NEXT STEPS

- Reflect on the types of distractions you listed and the reasons for them.
- Implement restrictions on "voluntary" distractions – email alerts, smartphone notifications, Facebook, visitors, etc. (I even have to turn off my computer screen sometimes.) Designate times for these activities so they will not interfere with your top priorities.
- Look at your work area – is it obvious what your number-one priority or project is?
- If not, designate non-intrusive areas for lower-priority projects., documents and materials. Give yourself the opportunity to work "in the moment."

-30-
TEN PRACTICAL TIPS FOR A LEAN WORKSPACE...OR TPTFALW, FOR SHORT

I know what you're thinking.

Those Lean Six Sigma "gurus" never have any real, practical advice to offer. They just talk about process design theory and supply chains and throughput analysis and Sigma the sea monster.

Nothing useful. Just acronyms and certifications and some guys named Deming and Shewhart and Toyoda and Goldratt. You know, take-it-or-leave-it yawner kind of stuff.

Well, think again. I'm about to blow your socks off – Lean Six Sigma style.

Today, I'm sharing 10 things – yes, that's two hands' worth of things – that you can do to create a Lean workspace. By that, I mean 10 ways you can employ basic Lean principles to improve your productivity and workflow at your desk. I assume that is valuable to you.

These are so practical and straight-forward, you can print out this blog and put it in your file labeled "common sense."

How do I know they work? Only because I tried them myself. Embarrassingly, it only took me 3 years working in my current environment to practice what I preach (after all, I am a Lean Six Sigma evangelist).

Now, are you ready to be healed? Read on, willing disciple!

1. Free up your keyboard and mouse – go wireless – the key Lean principle here is flexibility. This will improve your ability to use your limited workspace, adding to your responsiveness, productivity and flow. The wires often get in the way and limit how far you can move these devices, forcing you to keep them parked in the same place all the time. Before I went wireless, my mouse would barely stay in reach, because of the distance the wire had to travel to connect to my desktop. Very annoying.
2. Keep the things you frequently use close to you – certain files, supplies, telephone, notepad, etc. – and move everything else farther away. The principle here is "point-of-use" – keep things where they are used or needed, keeping them out of the way of other more important things. I have my frequently used files next to my monitor – keeping them top-of-mind and reducing the effort required to retrieve them. At a glance, I can tell what projects are on the front burner. I'm able to rotate my daily sales call files from front to back quickly and easily, allowing me quickly see whom to call today. This also employs the "flow" principle.
3. Stand up – literally! Yes, make or invest in a standing work station – you'll be amazed at the productivity difference, not to mention how much easier it is to move about, get to things, etc. Your back will also thank you. Plus, you'll find yourself in motion more easily, which naturally frees up the mind to be more

creative and alive. I keep a flip chart on an easel in a corner diagonal from where I stand, so I can quickly sketch out ideas or brainstorm when it starts to rain. Again, focusing on flow and velocity, and leveraging my creativity instead of stifling it.

4. Here's a look at my new standing work station:

Note that the computer and other "background" items are stored under the work area, allowing me to keep only active files close at-hand. Keyboard and mouse are wireless, and there is ample workspace. All necessary wires and cables are tucked away behind the desk. Another nice feature is having my printer/scanner/copier/fax within arm's reach. Not fully pictured is my L-return, where I can sit and work at my laptop when my feet get tired. Give yourself space to work – don't crowd your desk with everything from supplies to files – you can't flow if you can't move. Have a spot for working documents, and have a spot for waiting documents. The principle here is visibility and flow.

5. Stow away those wires! It's amazing how much of a mess the wires for even a basic office setup can create – just a desktop computer, monitor, printer, modem and other peripherals can easily require 10 cables and wires. Keep the wires out of walkways and away from heating fixtures. Tuck them neatly away behind your desk, grouping them together with twist-wires, if necessary. This also frees up space, reduces clutter and is more visually appealing. Again, enhancing flow, improving safety and optimizing your workspace.
6. Make your workday visible – Use a dry erase board to track what you need to do, what you're currently doing, and what's been done. Make sticky-notes for each deliverable and move it from "doing" to "done" as you proceed. Hang onto stickies for common tasks that you will repeat later. This gives clarity to your workload and helps you actually see the "flow" of things.
7. Don't stack things – this hides work and makes it unlikely you'll ever get to it. If you do have to stack, make regular time to work the stack – review what's there and take action on it. File it if you know you'll need it later. Otherwise, discard it. Here, you're minimizing WIP – work in progress – which can eventually sap your resources.
8. Keep a visible calendar. Ideally, this is a physical calendar, not one on your computer screen. Yes, I know it sounds redundant, but the key is to keep this important tool visible at a glance. Once you do, you'll be amazed how often you refer to it. What day of the week is it again? How many weeks are there in this month? Is Christmas on a Saturday this year? When's

my anniversary? Those are just a few of the burning questions you'll find yourself asking, and answering – all the while saving time and having information visible and available at the point-of-use. (Might even save your marriage.)

9. Use the walls for key job aids or company information. I have a medium-sized dry erase board to my left that shows the key talking points for my business (just in case I forget), important phone numbers and other items. It's a great assistant when I make cold calls. If I draw a blank, I just glance to my left to spark my memory (I know, it sounds odd). This not only makes this important information visible, but it also standardizes how I describe my business. It helps me stay on message, as they say. I also don't have to remember as much.

10. Organize your pencil cups! This may sound childish, but you'd be amazed how much time is wasted digging around in one of those things to find a pen that's the right color, or to simply find a pen instead of a pointer, screwdriver, fingernail file, miniature flag, spork, glue stick, tire gauge or similar device. They all seem to find their way into the cup. I've had to dedicate just one cup for pens and pencils, and another for everything else (which I rarely use). Makes it a lot easier to jot a quick note. There's nothing more frustrating (or embarrassing) than being on the phone with a client and forcing a pregnant pause as you scramble for something to write with. Do yourself a favor – make them easy to find and easy to put back. And when a pen runs out, by all means do not put it back in the cup. That will earn you 10 Lean

demerits and a lengthy lecture on the 1.5 Sigma shift. (Trust me, it'll just be better if you toss the sucker.)

That's it! You now have 10 commandments for a Lean workspace. Break them at your peril – the senseis are watching! But don't get too creeped out – they're probably too busy debating DMAIC vs. DMADV to notice.

Keep bustin'!

QUESTIONS TO CONSIDER

- What are the benefits of a "Lean" workspace?
- What is the difference between a "Lean" workspace and one that is simply "organized?"
- How does your workspace make you feel? Invigorated? Or burdened and overwhelmed?
- Are you able to find what you need, when you need it?
- Does everything have an assigned place, and a routine for returning it to that place?
- What types of waste does your workspace create?

NEXT STEPS

- Apply 2 of these 10 principles each week for the next 5 weeks.
- Find a way to stand up regularly or move about freely, even if you can't create a standing workstation.
- Note your improvement in productivity and mood.

-31-
LET YOUR LEAN LEGS DO THE WALKING

Always one for an adventure, my wife – a professional author and blogger, whose works you can find at www.charmainetdavis.com – recently decided to take on a seasonal job. She said it was to make a few extra bucks to buy me an extravagant anniversary gift (this year was our 20th); I suspected it was really to gather material for her latest novel; the funniest folks are right under our noses, she always says. While her reasoning smelled fishy to me, I played along.

Her seasonal job would have her out in the seasons, all right: she was to deliver Yellow Books to hundreds of locations in town – in person, on foot. Unfortunately, the season for this seasonal job was summer – the hottest one we've had in a long time. Rumor has it all painting jobs were canceled this year when the paint refused to dry.

Always one to lend a helping hand – particularly if it pays – I offered to help. I couldn't just let her roam the streets alone, without a crafty process engineer to guard her, could I? (Admit it; you would have done the same thing.) Seeing no resumes for such a person in my company files, I volunteered for the post. Plus, I'm a "seasoned" professional when it comes to deliveries (and, with 7 children, so is she). I've delivered everything from newspapers to pizzas to Census forms in my long, illustrious, logistics career. Yellow Books would be a piece of cake. Take the Books to the addresses on the map provided, rinse and repeat until all the Books are gone. (Trust me, after spending a hot and grimy day on the road, rinsing was definitely part of the process.) What could go wrong? Nothing, of course. Mr. Seasoned Process Engineer was on the scene.

Determined that this would be the Usain Bolt of all Yellow Book deliveries, I plotted a prudent and stealthy course the night before we set out. I was proud of that. Nothing does more to inflate a geek's pride than preparation. I marked up the maps, listed the destinations in logical order and went to bed higher than a kite from yellow highlighter fumes. My service to what we affectionately came to call "the Yellow Book of power" had begun. I had donated many brain cells – figuratively and literally – to the cause.

As I lay in bed, I gushed over the "charter" I had created for our project:

Objective:
- Deliver Yellow Books to every address listed on the manifest by the deadline

Goals:
- Move expediently from location to location
- Waste as little time and effort as possible
- Conserve energy
- Maximize hourly rate of compensation (we were being paid by the Book)

Requirements:
- Yellow Books must be inserted in clear plastic bag

- Yellow Books must be placed on hinge side of entry door
- Advertisers must be given two copies
- Advertisers must sign to confirm receipt
- GPS must be active during deliveries
- Manifest must be updated to show actual deliveries.

With such a tidy charter to guide us, what could possibly go wrong? The Mayflower Compact paled in comparison. And those guys did all right. Didn't they?

Yellow Books had to be removed from their shrink-wrapping and individually bagged for delivery.

Morning came. Our 4-door Mitsubishi Mirage loaded like a pack animal, we headed out like nomads into the rising sun, our pores teeming with sweat. We stuck to our seats. We shifted often. We tested the AC we suspected was dead, and found no pulse. Even so, we trudged on into the volcanic day, fixated like Frodo and Sam on the Mordor of our mission. We bore the "Yellow Book" of power.

It didn't take long to realize that the crafty process engineer I had hired had failed to incorporate one essential element into his process: the PROCESS. Who was supposed to do what? Were we going to park and both deliver Books? Who was going to bag those suckers, anyway? Who was going to keep track of where we'd been, so we wouldn't backtrack or double-up and commit the cardinal sin of redundancy?

Those were good questions. They screamed at me as loudly as the dump truck driver behind me when I failed to signal my intentions to ease off the road. So he signaled his intentions for me. It was a pleasant exchange. Let's just say he "plus-oned" me.

I consider my wife the boss (an affectionate nickname I have for her). As such, she would be the point person, the face to the customer, handling the bulk of the deliveries. I would be the support guy – you know, the glue in the operation.

Mr. Logistics.

Mr. Dead-Sweaty-Meat-If-I-Didn't-Figure-This-Process-Out-Quickly. You know, him.

Sketching like a madman with a nubby pencil on a crusty napkin, I had the plan:

Roles:

- Me: Driver, trip planner, navigator, tracker, bagger, stacker. The help.
- Her: Door-to-door delivery person. The boss.

Sounded good to me. I had the keys. She had the Books. No need to get her input. She had better things to do, like fending off all offers of cheap lemonade in Dixie cups from

entrepreneurial kids in Bermudas and tanks. I sketched on...
Process (small batch, level flow with a workflow trigger):

- Start with 5 bagged Yellow Books (includes a small buffer for any distractions the bagger experiences, including black-outs from heat exhaustion).
- Drive to first location (never mind the route; that's a story for another day).
- Delivery person (her) exit with two bagged Books.
- Driver cruise slowly along the side as the delivery person makes the drops.
- Mark off each address as the drops are made. I could do that. I was good at marking off things. And Mark's my name. I'm a natural.
- As the second drop is being made, bag two Books (one at a time) and replenish the floor board stock. I could do this, too. Kind of made sense, since I would be the one in the car.
- When the delivery person returns, they can pull the next two Books and walk to the next two houses, or ride to the next location.
- Continue this process until the back seat stock is down to, say, 10 Books. At that point, replenish the stock with Books from the trunk (Books and bags).
- Repeat until all the Books have been delivered.
- Collect massive amounts of Yellow cash. This is what we in process engineering land call the "dream" state.

Not bad, eh? The second leading cause of an overinflated geek ego is a clever process all broken down into myriad bullet points. Makes the hair on his toes curl. But not mine, of course. Just sayin'. Anyway...

So we did this. Took a little practice — and a lot of

explaining to the uninitiated – but what we did resembled what was written, most of the time. Sometimes one of us would ease into the other's role, if the situation demanded. (Not the driving bit; the other stuff.) And, of course, I raved about us having a pull process with a small batch size the whole way ... how it was making our lives easier, keeping the car uncluttered, minimizing frustration, keeping us moving (great for producing a constant breeze), etc. For those interested, here's the full inventory of benefits I reminded my wife of every time she reached for the keys:

Benefits:

- We only bagged as many Books as we needed.
- WIP (work in process) was kept to a minimum. Though, she did threaten to "WIP" me a few times.
- Bagged Books were not scattered all over the car.
- The delivery person could focus on deliveries (hint, hint).
- The delivery person was not slowed by bagging, navigating, documenting or re-supplying.
- The deliveries were not slowed for long periods of Book-bagging.
- There was always a bagged Book ready for the delivery person.
- The driver's time was optimized, not just spent driving, then waiting, driving, then waiting.
- Wait time was minimized for both resources. Value-added time was maximized. And we shared a lot of quality time, my wife and I.

Of course she agreed with it all. I know she did. I know when she said, "Why am I the one delivering all the Books? When do I get to drive?" that she really was just marveling about how wonderfully balanced our process was, and how easy it would be to shift from one role to the other, since it was so cleverly designed. But we didn't need to do that. Just knowing it was enough. After all, she was the boss, and I could never fill that role. My destiny was only to bear Frodo; hers was to bear the Yellow Book of power. It was a fellowship that could not be broken.

The Fellowship of the Lean.

_____QUESTIONS TO CONSIDER_____

- Have you ever felt the need to "process map" an activity that you thought would be routine? What were the results? Was it beneficial?
- When you're assigned a new task, do you tend to "figure it out as you go," or do you list or map out the steps first?

_____NEXT STEPS_____

- Choose a regular activity at work or home (e.g. cleaning the kitchen). Lead a group in mapping out the steps and responsibilities.
- Note the questions and ambiguities that are exposed.
- Make process mapping a regular way of determining, reviewing and clarifying roles and procedures.

-32-
HOW YA' DOIN'? HOW DO YA' KNOW?

One of our favorite phrases in America is "how ya' doing?" Because we say and hear it so often, we rarely listen to the answer or give one that is meaningful. It's just a way of acknowledging mutual existence, a recognition that another human has passed our way.

In our personal relationships, "how ya' doing" is simply a polite gesture. Sad to say, it doesn't really matter if we know the answer. In business, however, we have to know how we're doing. And the simplest, clearest indicator of how we're doing is how our customers think we're doing.

All too often, we take solace in silence and assume we're performing well. "No complaints, no problems," we naively believe. The flip side can also be true; we sometimes grade ourselves on the only feedback we get, and that typically is a complaint rather than praise. Unfortunately, people are more likely to give unsolicited complaints than compliments.

But neither of these sources is a valid indicator, simply because neither provides a representative sample of our customer base – which points to a key function a learning organization must have: an effective means of gathering valid performance data.

In the old days, a business would put a suggestion box in a waiting room or lobby and wait for the ideas to roll in. Notice I said "in the old days." We can't afford to sit around and wait for feedback anymore. Ever see anyone put anything in one of those boxes? Better yet, ever see anyone come and clean it out? At the end of the day, it's just a lazy way of acting like you care. People will give you their feedback by going next door to your competitor.

If we really care about our customers, we'll continually ask them how we're doing. We'll solicit their feedback without fear or repercussion. We must make it clear that we care about the answer. We must take no offense, but receive the feedback as constructive criticism, a customer's contribution to our ongoing enrichment.

There are many different ways to collect useful performance data:

- Train sales staff and service people to ask for feedback in non-leading ways.
- Ask for feedback after every customer engagement or product/service delivery.
- Ask, "What would have made your experience better?"
- Communicate the areas we are grading ourselves on. Ensure they match what our customers are grading us on, e.g. timeliness, responsiveness, effectiveness.
- Make performance standards measurable. We should ask, "How quickly do you need that?" Then we should measure how quickly we provide it on a regular basis.

- Formalize data-gathering in the form of surveys, questionnaires or written comment forms.

Most importantly, we must then do something with what we learn. Read the comments. Take them to heart. Affinitize them to identify areas of focus. Communicate the learnings to our teams. Assign owners to different indicators. Form teams to address problems. Let our customers know what we're doing.

The company that is able to take negative feedback and turn it into positive change is three steps ahead of its competition: 1) it's asking; 2) it's listening; and 3) it's doing. It may be a risk to ask for feedback, but the rewards come in the rich relationships with loyal customers and a business that reflects the heartbeat of its clients.

QUESTIONS TO CONSIDER

- How do you measure your company's success in meeting customer needs?
- Is profit the best indicator? Why or why not?
- Are your indicators leading or lagging?

NEXT STEPS

- Consider using a customer feedback mechanism you've never used before, e.g. focus groups vs. basic surveys.
- Capture takeaways and surprises. Share broadly.
- Recruit a team to address the negatives in priority order. Make this new "listening post" a standard exercise.

-33-
DO NOT ASK FOR WHOM THE DOOR SLAMS ... IT SLAMS FOR THEE

I spent some time observing in a rather large and busy community health clinic recently.

The facility, like most of its type, is not the most modern. The floors are worn. The colors are drab. The furnishings are 1980's-era, at the latest. And the aroma, well, let's just say the air doesn't circulate as freely as it needs to.

But all of those things were tolerable, largely because they are not unexpected in a practice that serves what is often referred to as the "underserved" in the community, applying a limited amount of resources to an ever-growing population.

The worst part

What eventually became intolerable, though, was the slamming of the heavy wooden office door, every time a patient, family member or staff member would enter or exit for any reason ... to use the phone, use the bathroom, take a break, sign in, head to the parking lot, etc. There would be a click, the quick turning and recoil of a metal knob, the audible swinging of a solid door that must have weighed 100 pounds, and then ... bam! The door would smack closed with a whack that was loud enough to wake the dead (as my Dad used to say).

Punch drunk

Once would have been OK – a little jarring, but bearable. Twice ... I would have stirred in my chair a bit, then resettled. But it went on and on, like mortars going off in a random pattern. My hair flew up with each slam. My ears began to ring. I started to develop some mild version of PTSD ... I developed a nervous twitch in my eyelid and I flinched every time someone got up. I shifted repeatedly in my chair. I began to pace about the room in a mock inspection of the magazine stacks. Eventually, I found myself wanting to put my hands over my ears and curl up in the corner, begging for someone to "just make it stop, please, make it stop..."

Is it just me?

I looked around to see if anyone else was bothered by the incessant smacking of the ancient door. Apparently, I was alone in my discontent. Mothers quietly redirected their children as they stacked (or threw) Lego blocks ... Young adults focused intently on their phone screens ... Elders picked and peeled their way quietly through the pages of various magazines ... Others just stared ahead blankly in quiet resolve.

Perhaps they were all regulars who had finally been deafened by the continual slamming of the giant nuisance.

What amazed me was not the presence of a massive door of doom in an aging medical facility. What I couldn't understand is why no one wanted to do anything about it.

People were constantly going in, and out, in, and out ... not a single one thinking to ease the door closed as they exited.

I almost expected a sign apologizing for the situation: "Please forgive us for the door. Please close gently so as not to disturb others." But no.

Instead it was as if everyone accepted it. The giant gorilla wasn't real if they chose to ignore it.

An ominous emblem

To me this is almost emblematic of our expectations of the healthcare experience in general. We wait and nobody cares. We make waiting rooms comfy and cozy and call it customer service. We get 5-10 minutes with our doctors and we feel lucky, as he scrawls out notes or clicks and types and hustles to the next. We take no steps — not even a door stop or spring-loaded hinge or pesky sign, for goodness sake — to address a slamming door. We let paint peel, floors wear and roofs leak.

Trust me, the "underserved" notice these things and believe they are intentional parts of a "second-class" system designed for them. The rest of society gets the good stuff. What's worse, there are even some care providers who have adopted this cynical attitude toward their "underprivileged" clients, for a variety of reasons.

Is this it?

Is this what we have come to in our healthcare system? Have we resigned ourselves to accepting what we would find intolerable in any other commercial enterprise?

And more alarmingly, and even more importantly, is this where we are going?

Something to think about...

QUESTIONS TO CONSIDER

- How would you have felt in this situation?
- What would have been your impression of the practice?
- Would you have felt uncomfortable?
- Would you have expressed concern?

NEXT STEPS

- Put yourself in the shoes of one of your customers. Go "undercover" as a mystery shopper, if need be.
- Take note of any "slamming doors" – sights, sounds, smells or experiences that make a negative impression. Include staff comments, accommodations, aesthetics, privacy and other often-overlooked aspects.
- Address any findings that could damage the customer experience or impression.
- Strive to create a "first-class" culture for your customers.

-34-
LAYMAN'S DEFINITION OF LEAN SIX SIGMA

At a high level, Lean Six Sigma is the decision that you're going to judge or measure your performance, and compare it to something meaningful, objective and far-reaching, and then take intentional steps to pursue "perfection."

Then comes the question – what to compare to?

At this point, you realize that:

- Your customers define your existence.
- They define what Quality means.
- Your Quality should vary as little as possible in their eyes, and objectively; and
- You should measure Quality the same way they do.

And so ultimately, Lean Six Sigma is the decision to define and measure Quality the same ways your customers do.

Lean Six Sigma, therefore, is not just a methodology, or a toolset, or a statistical measure ... it is a decision.

Have you made that decision yet?

Hello? Anybody there?

QUESTIONS TO CONSIDER

- How do your customers judge your performance? Have you ever asked them?
- Do your measures reflect what your customers feel is most important? Or are your internal metrics self-centered?
- Who or what determines what you measure, and how?

NEXT STEPS

- Make the decision to identify your customers' top priorities and measure how well you are meeting them.
- Eliminate other measures that are not grounded in your customers' priorities.

-35-
WHY ARE WE SATISFIED WITH WASTE?

It never ceases to amaze me how people can be satisfied with a bad workflow. In their own business, even.

Like it's going to magically fix itself somehow.

Like the money being wasted is not real money, the time being lost is not real time and the customers being disserved and dissatisfied are not real people.

Like it's just something you can just live with for awhile until every other priority has been taken care of. Or not.

How important is success? How important are our resources? Especially a resource like time, which cannot be recovered?

Are we just content with meeting low expectations? Afraid of aiming for something higher only to fail?

Is there safety in a bad workflow? Does waste cocoon us from dealing with real problems and real people? Does it demand great effort but little innovation and low accountability? Are the standards comfortably within our reach so that we would rather not change them?

I want to know.

Perhaps the answer is us?

Perhaps it's because we continue to accept junk mail in our mailboxes in growing amounts. Perhaps it's the 30-minute wait that we have decided is standard at the doctor's office or DMV or help desk. Or our willingness to pay $30 for jeans that should really cost $5, $5 for ½-gallon cartons of ice cream that are really only 1.75 quarts, $1 for 2-liter sodas that are really only 1.5 liters, and full price for plastic imitations of what should really be metal or wood? We accept less and call it more when Wal-Mart puts up a "Rollback" sign.

Yes, our willingness to accept second-rate products and service is largely to blame for the sub-par processes that generate them. Until we start demanding more and better value, we will never experience it.

QUESTIONS TO CONSIDER

- What internal failures do you continually tolerate?
- What waste do you ignore?
- Does waste tend to alleviate itself, or does it perpetuate?
- Why does waste and poor quality often go unchallenged?

NEXT STEPS

- Identify one area where waste is continually ignored.
- Lead the charge to identify the root cause and eliminate it.
- Keep asking, "Why does this happen" or "why do we let that happen," until the root cause becomes clear.
- Brainstorm solutions with a team.
- Do this continually at work and at home. Now you are a full-fledged waste-buster!

ABOUT THE AUTHOR

Mark H. Davis, a.k.a. process geek, super waste-buster and Lean Six Sigma evangelist, strives to put process improvement in the hands of the little guys.

Energized and energizing, he propels teams, executives and audiences to new heights of service and operational excellence with his passionate, witty and common-sense presentation of Lean Six Sigma. He knows this transformative improvement methodology from the inside-out, having trained, worked and taught others in the art of process improvement since 2000.

"Lean Six Sigma is an effective business philosophy for the masses, from the entrepreneur to the franchisee to the fry-dipper," he believes. "You don't have to have an endless string of capital letters after your name to use it. You only have to care about your customer and be willing to change whenever and however they say you should. Okay, so it might help if you can speak, reason and perform some basic math functions. And draw lines, straight as well as squiggly."

Specializing in healthcare performance improvement, Mark has consulted with medical practices, hospitals and health systems, as well as IT service providers, marketing agencies, insurance companies and others.

His regular musings can be found on the web at **www.workflowdiagnostics.wordpress.com** and **www.twitter.com/workflowdx**.

Mark is married to Charmaine T. Davis, who writes Christian fiction found on Amazon and other venues. He applies every ounce of his process improvement acumen to the raising of their seven children.

ACKNOWLEDGEMENTS

I would be remiss and distastefully prideful if I did not recognize how little of the credit for this work belongs to me. The following individuals deserve it all; I merely bear the fruits of their toils as they whittle away at my gangly branches and tend to my rocky soil:

Charmaine, for paving the way and proving it could be done;

Greg, for constant encouragement and seeing what I could not;

My kids, for patiently enduring all of the transitions of life that Daddy has put you through;

Members of the *Commonwealth Business Associates*, who nobly served as the test market for many of my newfangled ideas, and gently sharpened my dullness;

And Jesus my Lord, who has never forsaken me in my weakness. I love You above all.

www.ingramcontent.com/pod-product-compliance
Lightning Source LLC
LaVergne TN
LVHW051128080426
835510LV00018B/2295